Praise

'We accept that our cars need a regular service and MOT in order to perform effectively and safely. How do we manage to overlook the fact that our careers need the same attention? This book gives you a great set of tools to help you to regularly review and improve your personal performance at work.'
   — **Nicky Cowling**, Director, Good Day Yellow

'Watching the difference this makes to the development of people is fantastic and is a real testament to the programme. It works at all levels and helps not just individuals but organisational development as well.'
   — **Sue Davie**, Former Chief Executive, Meningitis Now

'There is no perfect company, organisation, manager, or colleague – you make your own happiness at work. This book provides a valuable and practical guide to making the most of your potential at work, challenging you to be the best you can and providing tools and techniques to support you in that endeavour.

'My client chose this programme when their company was about to enter a period of significant change. They had great staff and knew that they needed and wanted to retain as many of them as possible through the journey. Using this programme, we were able to encourage individuals to take stock of their careers and take charge of their own destiny resulting in a strong retained team with renewed vigour for the challenges ahead. Guided by the programme, some decided that it was time to continue to develop their careers in different directions, either by pursuing training for an enhanced role or to take advantage of new opportunities elsewhere.

'Our experience shows that by following this programme, particularly through a period of significant business change, your staff will be encouraged to perform to their very best, act responsibly and make their own, and your business's success.'

— **Ann George**, Director, Clarity Matters

The Pioneer

A powerful blueprint for greater success in your life and career

Ali Stewart & Dr Derek S Biddle

R^{e}think

This edition published in Great Britain in 2024 by Rethink Press (www.rethinkpress.com)

First published in 2018 under the title *Pioneering Professional*

© Copyright Ali Stewart & Dr Derek S Biddle

All rights reserved. No part of this publication may be reproduced, stored in or introduced into a retrieval system, or transmitted, in any form, or by any means (electronic, mechanical, photocopying, recording or otherwise) without the prior written permission of the publisher.

The right of Ali Stewart and Dr Derek S Biddle to be identified as the author of this work has been asserted by them in accordance with the Copyright, Designs and Patents Act 1988.

This book is sold subject to the condition that it shall not, by way of trade or otherwise, be lent, resold, hired out, or otherwise circulated without the publisher's prior consent in any form of binding or cover other than that in which it is published and without a similar condition including this condition being imposed on the subsequent purchaser.

Cover image © Ali Stewart & Co Ltd

One-line illustrations courtesy of Rob Lee
www.robotoon.com

Contents

Foreword	1
Introduction	3
1. The Crux	7
Part 1: The Mirror	9
Part 2: The Mindset	25
2. The Steps	41
Three Critical Steps	43
3. The Skills: Preparing for Increased Personal Excellence	59
Skill 1: Develops Personal Excellence	61
4. The Secrets: Positioning Yourself Well for Success	85
Skill 2: Seeks Clarity – why, what and how?	87
Skill 3: Negotiates for Success	107
Skill 4: Builds Strategic Business Acumen	121
5. The Gear Change: Performing at a Higher Level	131
Skill 5: Controls Own Workload	133
Skill 6: Manages Own Learning	141
6. The Impact	159
Skill 7: Takes Charge of Own Career	161
The Review: Putting it all together	177

Bibliography	185
Other Books In The Series	187
Next Steps: The Pioneer Programme	193
Acknowledgements	195
The Authors	197

Foreword

Advancements in robotics and artificial intelligence are refining the workplaces of today, while defining how they will look tomorrow. Increasingly, success is less about what skills you possess, and more about how you choose to deploy them. As the world embraces the next generation of technological advancement, people of quality, those with unique skills, are much in demand.

What separates you, from the many? What guarantees you, your job, tomorrow? The answer is surprisingly simple: it is increased self-awareness with greater emotional and spiritual intelligence.

The Pioneer provides a simple and highly effective tool kit. Firstly, a mindset and secondly, a set of rules to follow that have unlocked what you already know. How do you attain excellence in both leadership and followership?

You've realised already that it is about deploying the right steps at the correct time. *The Pioneer* provides a framework, a formula for deploying your knowledge into bite-sized deliverables of excellence. You know at the core is you. Understanding who you really are and the palpable impact you have on others is a critical first step. Recognise, realise and redefine your potential.

In your hand is the second book of a 'terrific trio': *The Seeker*, a bite-sized introduction as to 'why bother?'; *The Pioneer*, to raise you to higher heights and develop your own unique style, and then *The Liberator*, to give you the explicit leadership skills that schools forget to teach.

This is a practical book, with working pages to help you work on you. Annotate, sketch and highlight with gusto as you read and re-read; make these skills your very own.

Good luck, savour this moment and remember to enjoy your journey!

Adam Tuffnell, Managing Director,
Onefathom Limited

Introduction

What makes highfliers fly? How is it that some people become very successful very quickly, they get promoted earlier than most, and yet at the same time they seem to have a great life outside work? Why is it that other people who work hard struggle to achieve the same success? How do you lift yourself up and demonstrate the kind of Personal Excellence that really effective people display?

We set about researching this in a major UK organisation and became excited by the results. Then we carried on researching and testing in a range of other organisations, big and small, in the public and private sectors. The findings were the same. Our research demonstrated that what differentiated the successful, effective people from others who were less effective, was The Mindset they had, and 7 Key Skills.

The effective people had naturally acquired The Mindset and Skills, and it had nothing to do with having a high IQ. It had more to do with EQ (Emotional Intelligence), taking charge of your own learning and life, and being self-directing. The exciting part is that these Skills can be studied and acquired by anyone.

This is supported by all the recent champions and authors of self-development like Daniel Goleman[1] (author of *Emotional Intelligence*), who said:

> 'The good news is that emotional intelligence can be learned. Individually we can add these skills to our tool kit for survival at a time when "job security" seems like a quaint oxymoron... having these capabilities offers each of us a way to survive with our humanity and sanity intact, no matter where we work. And as the work changes, these human capacities can help us not just compete, but also nurture the capacity for pleasure, even joy, in our work.'

And a fabulous champion of self-improvement, Dale Carnegie, said:

> 'Fifteen percent of your earning potential comes from knowledge and direct skills, the other eighty-five percent comes from leadership and interpersonal skills.'[2]

---

1 Goleman, D, *Emotional Intelligence* (Bantam Books, 2006)
2 Carnegie, D, *How To Win Friends And Influence People* (Vermillion, 2006)

So, understanding and practising The Mindset and Skills of *The Pioneer* is key to developing your own Personal Excellence. We will lead you through a process for doing just this; it is a journey we invite you to come on with us.

This workbook includes tools and questionnaires for you to assess and expand your thinking. You can learn what makes the highfliers fly, and acknowledge and brush-up the fine skills you already possess.

6-Point Plan

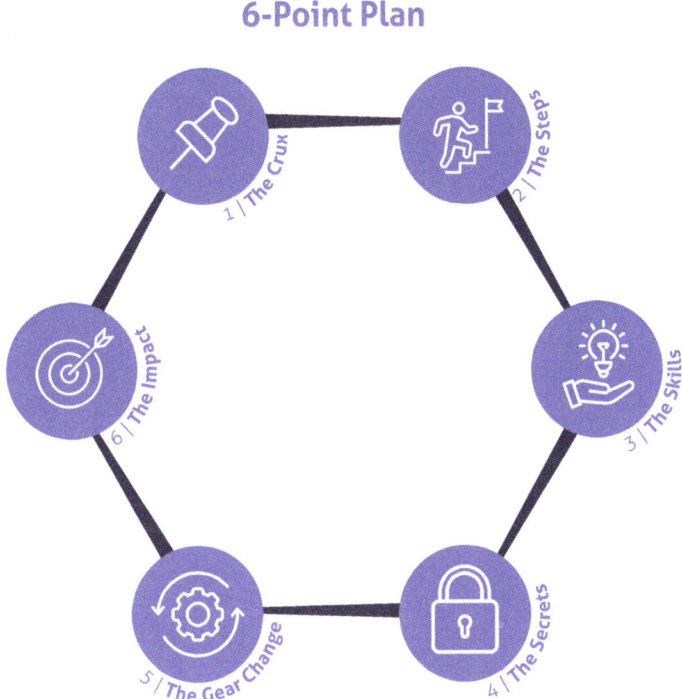

The Pioneer is the second in our series of three books. In our first book, *The Seeker*, we introduced a 6-Point Plan to guide you through things. We are going to do the same here, to help your learning journey through the Mindset and Skills of *The Pioneer*.

Are you ready? We'll start with a stock take of how you are doing right now.

THE CRUX

PART 1: The Mirror
Understands self and others
Jungian theory explained
Bringing the theory to life
Why understanding yourself and others matters

PART 2: The Mindset
Are you a Work Victim or Pioneer?
So whose business is it anyway?
Our development as people
The Mindset and behaviours of The Pioneer
Chapter summary

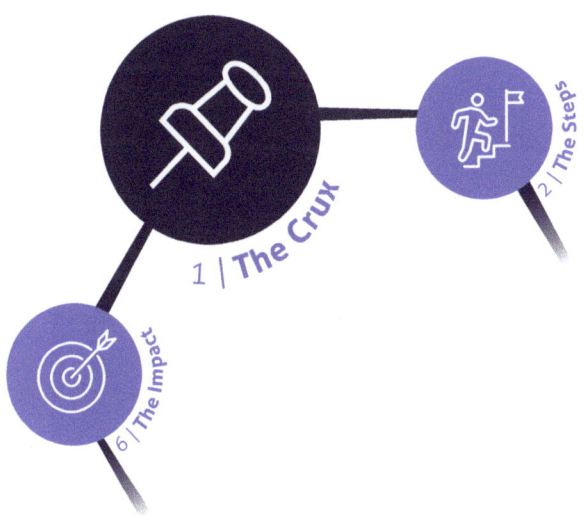

'Success isn't a result of spontaneous combustion. You must set yourself on fire.'
— Arnold H Glasgow

Part 1: The Mirror

Understands self and others

The Pioneer's approach is to be perceptive about themselves. They hold up the mirror in every way they know how and take a long, hard look. This is always the starting point.

They deploy their strengths well and face up to their weaknesses, finding ways to manage them instead of just denying or ignoring them. The more competent people are, the more they are conscious of the diversity of other people, their strengths and corresponding weaknesses, and are able to recognise and work with their strengths. We call this Interdependence, which we will be talking a lot more about, where the diversity and capacity of others is acknowledged and used productively.

A common problem for many is that, when people are not like us, we tend to see their weaknesses and not their strengths. We are drawn to people who are more like us, those who share the same kind of outlook on life, the same values, who are similar in thinking on a range of issues. We tend to regard them as reliable, likeable, honest and true. When thinking about those who are not like us, who have opposing thoughts, values, ways of working and ways of thinking, we can often regard them as more unreliable, unlikeable, annoying and frankly wrong – especially on those stressful days when we are not in a resourceful state and our patience and resilience is low.

> 'If one does not understand a person,
> one tends to regard him as a fool.'
> — Dr Carl G Jung

Another problem is that we are never taught the kind of self-leadership and interpersonal skills we need in life. At school, we learn knowledge and direct skills. These skills are prized above all others. We are trained for a university education; we might come through the system with a degree in a subject or skill and get on because of our technical competence. The kind of interpersonal skills we need are often called 'soft skills' and traditionally have been frowned on, with leaders in organisations seeing the real work being connected with the task, and with outputs and bottom-line performance.

Times are changing, and being able to get on with people is seen as a desired characteristic. It is a key quality of our Pioneers to understand themselves and others, and it takes courage to take a long, hard look at yourself. Some people are too frightened and they hide behind tasks and getting the job done.

PART 1: THE MIRROR

'People will do anything, no matter how absurd, to avoid facing their own souls.'
— Dr Carl G Jung

Developing your competence in this area is therefore key. Psychometric tools offer a way of discovering what you are like, a way of holding up the mirror for you to really see yourself. Such tools seek to understand the mind, and, of course, with the mind, there is no right or wrong, each person is unique.

Many psychometric tools are based on the pioneering work of Swiss psychologist Dr Carl G Jung, the Myers Briggs Type Indicator (MBTI) being one, Insights Discovery® another, Clarity4D another – there are many more. They are of significant help to you in assessing your own strengths and areas that need development, as well as recognising and understanding those of others.

Right here, right now, over the next few pages, we are going to share with you a quick way of assessing yourself, to get you started.

Since ancient times, philosophers have identified four broad types of personality. Carl Jung further developed this idea in the twentieth century. He suggested that all personality types are present in all of us, and the different balances between them are what make us unique.

Jungian theory explained

Jung suggested we have two distinct attitudes in the way we express ourselves, which he called Extraversion and Introversion. Just to be clear, Extraversion in the Jungian sense is not just about being loud, and Introversion is not about being shy. Although Extraverts are generally louder, Introverts can be loud when they need to be. And although some Introverts can be shy, so too can Extraverts. Both attitudes are dynamic and are typically viewed on a single continuum. See how you get on with the statements which follow. Put a mark on the horizontal line showing how much of each indicator is present for you. The shaded area in the middle is out of bounds – decide which side of the shading is more like you.

INTROVERSION		EXTRAVERSION
Holds back	↔	Bold
Quieter voice tone	↔	Louder voice tone
Stands back and observes	↔	Engages and speaks
Good listener	↔	Dominates conversation
Lives in inner world	↔	Lives in outer world
Reflective	↔	Expressive
E-mail or text	↔	Phone call
Easily distracted	↔	Easily bored
Values depth of knowledge	↔	Values breadth of experience
Calm	↔	Excitable

If you are more Extraverted, you will typically have a louder voice tone, and use more gestures. You are likely to be more action-oriented and bold. People will know what you think of them because it probably shows on your face. Extraverts 'speak to think' – they tend to toss ideas out to the world, to get a response to know if it's true. They love to have a breadth of knowledge, knowing a little about a lot of things, and have a gift for talking with great authority when they only know a little about something. Often, they wonder how they get away with it, but because they say it with authority, people believe them. 'Gift of the gab' as it is sometimes called! Extraverts can appear too brash and assertive to more Introverted types.

If you are more Introverted, you will typically have a quieter voice tone and use fewer gestures. You are likely to be more reflective and listen well. People rarely know what you are thinking, because it doesn't show on your face, and the only way people can know is if they ask you. Introverts 'think to speak' – they don't like to say anything unless they know it to be true. They will tend to keep quiet if they don't understand something, preferring to go and find out about it later, on their own. They like to have a depth of knowledge and will only talk with great authority when they know all about a subject. At such times they can appear quite Extraverted, sure of their knowledge. Introverts can appear too quiet and dull to more Extraverted types.

You may have a more even distribution between the two ends of the scale. You may see others who are more outgoing and sociable than you, and you may know others who are more reserved and quiet than you. There are people all along the continuum; that's what makes us diverse and interesting. Read on, the extremes which follow may have more of a marked impact on you.

Carl Jung also identified in us four functions:

1. Thinking
2. Feeling
3. Sensing
4. Intuition

The first two are *rational* functions, called Thinking and Feeling. They are rational because they are the way we judge things and make decisions and are usually visible to others. As before, they are shown on a continuum. See how you get on with the statements below to suggest whether your preference is more toward Thinking or Feeling. Again, the shaded area in the middle is out of bounds – decide which side of the shading is more like you.

If you are more Thinking, you focus more on the task. Decisions are based on logic and data. Your thinking is analytical and objective, and if all data points to a particular course of action, that is what you will do: it's the only logical way to go. You like to be appreciated for your sound reasoning and ability to make

THINKING

- Task oriented
- Logical
- Looks at data
- Frank
- More cold and objective
- Impersonal
- Critical
- Tough-minded
- Detached
- Rational

FEELING

- People oriented
- Harmonious
- Looks at relationship
- Tactful
- More warm and compassionate
- Gentle
- Easily hurt
- Sensitive
- Personal
- Emotional

PART 1: THE MIRROR

a decision based on fact. You seek to create clear value, and your interactions with others are focused and business-like. You think with your head... and it can sometimes be difficult for you to recognise the Feeling function as valid as it seems so much woollier and more intangible.

If you are at the more Feeling end of the spectrum, you focus more on relationships. Decisions are accommodating and values-driven, based on a gut feeling. You are more sociable and crave a harmonious environment in which people get along. You like to be appreciated for the special contribution you make towards the well-being of others. Interactions are friendly, avoiding any conflict. People are more important than material things. You 'think' with your heart... and at times you struggle to appreciate the Thinking function because it seems so cold and calculating.

You may have a more even distribution between the two ends of the scale. It might be easier for you to lead with your Thinking function, for example, and look at the logic and data first, before you consider the impact on others and bring in your more accommodating, values-driven Feeling function... or maybe it is the other way round for you. For those with a distinct preference, it is obvious to others the way they make decisions. For those whose preferences are more finely balanced, others may not know how you are going to react to a situation unless you understand things and can explain your decision-making process.

Moving on, there are two *irrational* functions, Sensing and Intuition. In the Jungian sense, they are irrational because they flow from the unconscious and are without logic, often more difficult to spot in others, and indeed ourselves. However, they can have a powerful impact because they are the way we perceive everything. Again, they are shown on a continuum. See how you get on with the final set of statements below, to check whether your preference is more toward Sensing or Intuition. Once again, the shaded area in the middle is out of bounds – decide which side of the shading is more like you.

If you are at the more Sensing end of this spectrum, you pay more attention to information coming in through your five senses. If something new comes into your world, you need to be able to see it, hear it, taste it, smell it, touch it. For you, things need to be real and tangible. You take account of your physical surroundings. You notice facts and details and remember things like names, places, faces, important dates, what someone was wearing the last time you saw them, the colour of the wallpaper in a room, where people were sitting or what someone said. Sometimes you pay so much attention to detail, either in the past or what is going on in the here and now, that you miss new opportunities. Sometimes it is difficult for you to value the Intuitive function... for you, those higher in Intuition seem to have their head in the clouds, and sometimes what they say just doesn't make sense.

SENSING

- Practical
- Experience
- Highly organised
- Five senses
- Sees what actually happened
- Real and grounded
- Concrete
- Lives in present
- Goes by senses
- Notices details

INTUITION

- Theories
- Vision
- More chaotic
- Imagination
- Sees meaning behind what happened
- Fanciful and wild
- Abstract
- Lives in world of possibility
- Idealistic
- Notices mood

If you are more intuitive, you pay more attention to the patterns and possibilities that you see in the information you receive. You focus more on the future than the past and imagine how things might be. You love working with abstract theories and you solve problems by leaping between different ideas and possibilities. Sometimes these leaps are made in your head and you have a deep sense of knowing about things and get lost in your thoughts. Sometimes they just come to you and you shout about them. You like to do new, different things, excited by the big picture and new shiny opportunities. Sometimes you think so much about new possibilities that you miss what is going on in the here and now. It can be difficult for you to relate to the Sensing function... for you, those higher in Sensing just need to get a life; why can't they 'see' things? Why can't they dream big?

Bringing the theory to life

By combining the Attitudes of Extraversion and Introversion with the two rational, decision-making functions, Thinking and Feeling, we can start to see four broad personality types emerging, like this:

- **A combination of Extraversion and Thinking.** When paying attention, you are more competitive, assertive and demanding. Under moderate pressure, your anger may flare because you want action. You have a more directing style, love to be in control, install structure and process and drive for results.

- **A combination of Introversion and Thinking.**
When paying attention, you are more detail-conscious, analytical and correct. Under moderate pressure, you may become colder and nitpicky. Accuracy of information is of overriding importance; you love to take the time to think things through and get things right.

- **A combination of Extraversion and Feeling.**
When paying attention, you are more sociable, responsive and enthusiastic. Under moderate pressure, you may become more frantic and hasty. With irrepressible good humour and friendliness, you tend to light up every room you enter and inspire and engage others.

- **A combination of Introversion and Feeling.**
When paying attention, you are more patient, relaxed and nurturing. Under moderate pressure, you may withdraw and become stubborn. Your compassion for others is palpable, you are a great listener and get things done quietly and calmly.

With Sensing and Intuition flowing from the unconscious, without logic, they are much more difficult to measure. However, this is how they might combine with Extraversion and Introversion, giving eight broad types.

- **A combination of Extraversion and Sensing.**
  When paying attention, you are more organised, realistic and busy. Under moderate pressure, you may become agitated when there is chaos. You love tidying up and getting things done, and you are known for being incredibly practical, here and now, grounded.

- **A combination of Introversion and Sensing.**
  When paying attention, you are more correct, painstaking and reliable. Under moderate pressure, you will vociferously stand your ground. You have a keen eye for detail, you remember things that others forget, and you draw on your learning to date to make sense of the current situation.

- **A combination of Extraversion and Intuition.**
  When paying attention, you are more fast, excited and engaged. Under moderate pressure, you will double your speed – a rollercoaster ride! You are alert to opportunities, attracted by the next big challenge, not afraid to take chances, and inspired by success and freedom.

- **A combination of Introversion and Intuition.**
  When paying attention, you are knowing, visionary and insightful. Under moderate pressure, you will get lost in your own thoughts and become unfocused. You have a deep understanding and connection with others and with life. You see things like a prophet who just knows things, and is often intriguingly correct.

PART 1: THE MIRROR

These *irrational* functions combine with the four broad types listed previously to add a powerful level of depth and quality, leading to a huge variety of personality types.

Have you decided which type is more like you? Maybe you could ask a family member or work colleague to assess the Jungian scales for you and give you some feedback. Do they see the same as you see in yourself, or something different?

All personality types are equally valid, and we all have access to them all. In some organisations, it is noticeable that some types are prized over others, and you will know what it is like where you work. However, The Pioneer approach is to make use of all styles, because you then have the greatest connection with others. The highest performing leaders, too, have to tap into all types at different stages in the leadership process – one size or type does not fit all situations.

For more information, in my book *The Seeker*, I describe the powerful Insights Discovery® model, which brings the broad combinations to life through colour. Because the mind loves colour and patterns, this helps to make everything memorable and accessible and gives people a powerful language for communication, which can change cultures and lives.

Why understanding yourself and others matters

There are some other powerful reasons for understanding yourself and others better. These include:

- Giving you insight into what kind of work and situations suit you best, so you can be more successful and fulfilled

- Helping you understand and resolve difficulties with other people, including so-called but inappropriately named 'personality clashes'

- Discovering perhaps dormant talents that you have, which have yet to be exploited and fulfilled

- Developing the emotional competences or interpersonal skills to deal with other people effectively

As everyone is a leader of their own life, if you take responsibility for it, you will understand how to deploy your expertise and achieve increasing success. Remember, effective achievers are perceptive about themselves.

Part 2: The Mindset

Are you a Work Victim or a Pioneer?

Developing The Mindset of The Pioneer, as identified in our research, is of fundamental importance before you start learning The Skills. If you start learning The Skills without The Mindset, you will not go as fast or as far, will possibly go from job to job, and you may not feel truly fulfilled.

First, let's establish if you are a Work Victim or a Pioneer.

Consider the following situation.

> **Case study: Julian, the Work Victim**
>
> Julian had looked forward to his new job and to a successful career with this organisation. He expected steady promotion and a lifetime of satisfying, interesting and responsible work using the expertise he had worked so hard to gain. But it wasn't like that at all.
>
> There was always plenty to do, which meant Julian felt he was chasing his tail most of the time and could never get on top of things. He took instructions diligently but often found that he'd embarked on a

frustratingly wrong course of action once he'd been given a task. His manager always seemed busy and didn't devote enough time to Julian's development and career. Encouragement and attention were in short supply, although people were friendly enough.

Julian felt he could do more challenging work, but he didn't really know how to, and anyway, he might make mistakes or increase his workload. He did take on a project once but tripped over some of the political nuances rife in the organisation and the project wasn't a real success.

These days, Julian often feels he has to work in the dark and guess at what is required of him, only to be hit by totally unexpected problems. Besides, everything seems to change all the time, and as soon as he grasps a situation it somehow moves on to something different.

Julian has had some direct contact with clients, but they seem not to want to hear about his depth of knowledge and elegant solutions, but simply to get their own needs satisfied. Although it might cost more, Julian feels frustrated that such people can't see and appreciate what is on offer.

In the end, Julian has lost heart. His enthusiasm has waned, although out of necessity he still puts in long hours. He feels stressed and powerless and has little energy outside work to do the things he thought he wanted to do. He marks time, waiting for an opportunity to arise where life could be better. Meanwhile, there is yet another organisational change due. He will wait and see what fate has in store for him.

PART 2: THE MINDSET

> Julian has become a Work Victim. It is not a good place to be. It may be comfortable in the sense that the responsibility is seen by Julian to lie elsewhere, and he can't do very much about it except reduce his expectations and settle for a 'quiet' life. However, it is not a very secure, satisfying or rewarding place to be. Rather it has its own stresses, frustrations and dissatisfactions. No one gains, least of all Julian.

Complete the following quick self-assessment to see where you are on the Work Victim scale. Answer honestly. The totals at the end of each column will tell their own story – it needs little interpretation.

If you ticked 'Strongly Agree' or 'Agree' for ten or more of the assessment statements, you may well be on the way to becoming a Work Victim.

Time to take back control of your own life.

Success is not about waiting for the...

- **Perfect manager:** There aren't any. Many are good, but most are busy, and it is highly unlikely that any will be as interested in your success and career as you are.

- **Perfect organisation:** Again there aren't any. Some are clearly better than others, but the 'grass is greener' syndrome is often a trap.

Work Victim scale

	Tick the relevant box for each statement	Strongly Agree	Agree	Disagree	Strongly Disagree
1	I have little control over the way my work is done.				
2	I get little satisfaction from the work I do.				
3	The people who get in the way of me achieving real success are my managers.				
4	I feel stressed most of the time I'm at work.				
5	My contribution is not well recognised.				
6	There is little opportunity to learn new skills around here.				
7	No one takes any interest in my career.				
8	Things were much better in the 'old' days.				
9	I feel frustrated and powerless.				
10	I don't really know what I want to do in the future.				
11	I don't know how to achieve my aims.				
12	I feel that others less able than me succeed faster.				
13	I'm not in control of what happens to me.				
14	The demands made on me are impossible.				
15	I'm bored, under-stretched and under-utilised.				
16	I'm always having to fight the system or my manager.				
17	I'm not appreciated properly.				
18	I don't really know what is expected of me.				
19	My strengths aren't recognised and used.				
20	Other employers provide much better opportunities.				
	Total number of responses for each column				

PART 2: THE MINDSET

- **Perfect environment:** Same news again, some are better than others, but none are perfect.
- **Perfect job:** Some people spend a lifetime hoping to come across this. They rarely do.

It is like waiting for the perfect world: it hasn't happened yet, at least not over the last 4,000 years. It may happen sometime in the next 4,000. Are you prepared to wait, or would you rather make the best use of what is available to you right now? This brings us back to the research we mentioned in the introduction, and to The Mindset that distinguished the people who succeeded in work and life. They took responsibility for creating their own success through managing their own environment. They were self-directing. Those who lacked The Mindset saw themselves as passive victims of their environment, having everything done unto them, like this:

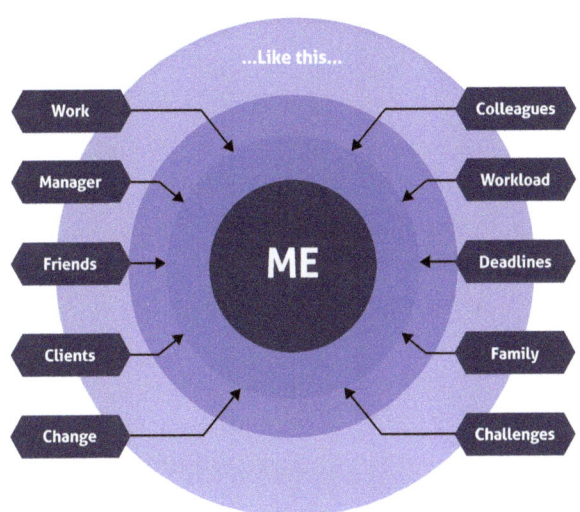

In contrast, those with The Mindset saw themselves as being in control, and shaping their own environment, like this:

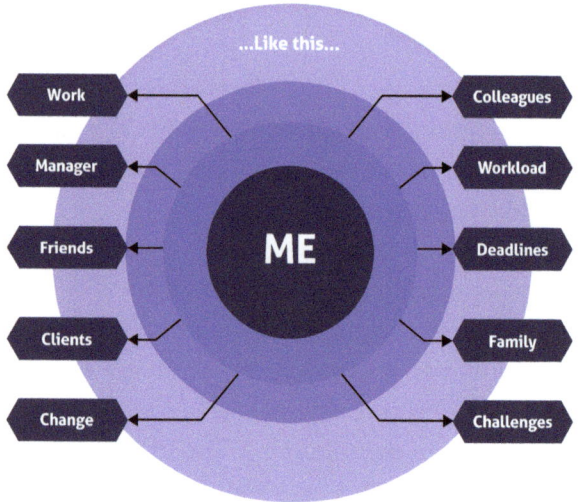

So whose business is it anyway?

The Pioneer sees themselves as managing their own business. Their business is them. Pioneers in employment, like the majority of us, operate a business within a business. They realise that no one cares as much about their own success as themselves, and that operating this way leads to win-win outcomes for everyone.

Most of us work for a living, unless we were born with the proverbial 'silver spoon', have a rich aunt, have a truly entrepreneurial streak or win the lottery! For many people, security comes from our employability, the value-added skills we have to offer in the marketplace. One aspect of self-directing behaviours is to keep such skills current. If you don't invest in your own business, how can you expect other people to do so?

Operating a business within a business puts a perspective on your life at work and on taking responsibility for yourself to achieve what you want. At one level this may be security. At another it may be promotion, or money, also achieved from a platform of being excellent at what you do. For many people, it is the satisfaction and achievement of excellently doing interesting, useful work.

As well as this, your business is not just the work part of it, but life overall. Do you want to manage this part of your business so you really get what you want, to have excellence outside work as well as within, or perhaps to strike the right balance between the two? The principles and Skills of The Pioneer will be of great value in life generally, which is an added bonus.

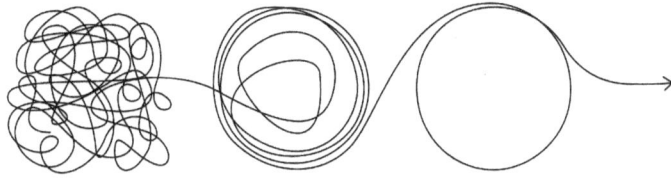

Our development as people

When you start to understand and embrace The Mindset of highly successful people, it is useful to look at a model for the way people tend to develop.

As babies and children, we are entirely Dependent on others to feed, clothe and nurture us. Part of growing away from this state can result in teenage rebellion or Counter-Dependency, where we test our boundaries and discount what others have told us. This, with any luck, is followed by early adulthood, where we have evolved a sense of who we are and what matters to us. We also feel sufficiently competent to deal with most of life and to function OK in the world, although our main preoccupation is still ourselves. We see ourselves as Independent people, responsible to ourselves.

The next significant stage is maturity, where we are no longer just Independent, making our own informed decisions and coping well. Now we have the capability to operate at another level, co-operating well with other people from the security of our own platform of self-worth, capable of taking their needs into account and proactively managing our own environment. This is Interdependence; we make choices rather than being driven by events or conditioning.

We can sum up the four stages like this:

Dependency	Being directed, nurtured and sustained by others
Counter-dependency	Being rebellious, taking irresponsible initiative, being preoccupied with self
Independency	Taking care of self, becoming inner-directed and self-reliant, thinking own thoughts, making own decisions
Interdependency	Being self-reliant, proactive and capable, but also being able to join with other people and share resources productively

Not all people make this journey to its full extent, of course. Some get stuck permanently in Dependency, either by choice or as a coping mechanism; a few are permanently rebelling; others are self-sufficient Independents who don't make the next step to embrace the potential richness of others.

Often, there is a dissonance between a person's behaviour inside work and their behaviour outside of it. Frequently, this is because of expectations: expectations that one will be told exactly what to do and be directed, that the manager will be there to take care of all needs, and in fact they are paid to do so. This view is often reinforced by managers under the 'command and control' system that some still use. People get habituated to this state of 'if that's what they want, that's what they'll get', and the 'jobsworth' enters the scene. Other people see themselves as pursuing meaningless or boring jobs and don't invest themselves psychologically in their work. Others, by default or design, find their fulfilment outside work. What happens too frequently these days, is that people are suddenly required to operate in an Interdependent, empowered fashion overnight. This is scary, and a not uncommon response is to stay with what is familiar, particularly if the person is not sure the organisation really means what it says.

These are just some of the reasons which sometimes inhibit people from operating to their full abilities. They may or may not apply to you, but, once the choices are made clear, most people elect to strive towards an Interdependent way of life.

The Mindset and behaviours of The Pioneer

Let's now identify more closely The Mindset and its resulting behaviours, as demonstrated by the highly effective people we have described. We'll start by getting what they are *not* out of the way!

Firstly, they are not Dependent 'subordinates':

- Dependent people take on a strongly subordinate role. They take all their problems to their manager and expect their manager to solve them. They wouldn't even think about trying to solve a problem for themselves. Rather they like being told what to do. They depend on others to manage them, their work and their needs.

- Dependent people are relatively powerless people who tend to blame others and the situation for any difficulties they encounter. They are not self-starters and often see themselves as 'victims' of a situation. Their manager is likely to see them as weak and ineffective.

Secondly, they are not Counter-Dependent 'subordinates':

- Over-independent or Counter-Dependent people also take on a subordinate role. They see a problem, decide that this is a chance to prove themselves by doing things their own way, and fail to keep their manager or colleagues appropriately informed. They ignore the wider view and are dismissive of others' inputs. Their solutions are often not good quality ones.

- In the manager's eyes, the Counter-Dependent subordinate resists control, thinks that they know it all, seeks personal glory and doesn't appreciate the manager's needs. Because of their over-independence, managers don't trust them and supervise them closely to head off trouble. They show lots of initiative, too much in fact, but little sense of real responsibility.

We have called both these two types of behaviour 'subordinate' behaviour because they cause the manager to feel the need to supervise them closely.

Interestingly, they are not Independent either:

- Independent people tend to be good corporate citizens. They try and do what is right in a responsible way. They are engaged with their work and focus on their tasks, but they often feel swamped by their workload and it's sometimes difficult to get their head above the horizon. They could take on more interesting, challenging work but find getting the balance right quite difficult.

- Independent people often identify strongly with the technical issues they face. They are skilled and clear in presenting problems to their managers. They tend to be obliging and courteous and help others when asked to do so. Sometimes they wonder why their conscientiousness isn't better recognised – for example, they notice that other people tend to make a greater impact and are promoted earlier. Often, they feel they are taken for granted. Although they put in the effort and are willing to relate to other people, and put in a good performance, this performance seldom achieves an 'excellent' level. Their life outside work is OK, but sometimes they wonder whether they could make more of the opportunities life has to offer.

So what *are* they? They are Interdependent, self-directing people – they are Pioneers.

- Interdependent Pioneers see a problem and take responsibility for ensuring it is dealt with. They present solutions not problems. They take responsibility for creating their own success, managing their own environment and working with others in a proactive and genuine way. In dealing with situations they take the broad view, asking themselves 'If this were my company, what would I do?' which necessarily includes taking the needs of everyone into account.

What are the crucial key differences between these four ways of operating? They are to do with initiative and taking responsibility for doing so, in a way which we describe as:

RESPONSIBLE INITIATIVE

For example:

- Dependent people don't use initiative: they rely passively on other people. Nor do they accept responsibility for themselves.

- Counter-Dependent people seize the initiative but use it irresponsibly, regardless of other people and the wider implications.

- Independent people use initiative but in a limited way within self-imposed boundaries, restricting their own capability. They are respectful of responsibility and accept it, but often limit how much they proactively manage their own situation. Most people tend to operate in this way, both at work and in their lives generally.

- Interdependent, self-directing people take personal responsibility for creating their own success and managing their own environment, using Responsible Initiative to do so.

> **TOP TIP**
>
> Having a self-directing orientation based on Responsible Initiative is the single most important aspect of being in control of one's own life and success. It differentiates people who are effective and who achieve excellence from those who are less effective.

Responsible Initiative is all about The Mindset of The Pioneer. Of course, this Mindset has to be backed up by a sound process and the 7 Key Skills which we will look at in the next chapter. What matters most is having The Mindset and ability, and to put it into practice. This book will help you to do that.

Chapter summary

Part 1: The Mirror

The Pioneer:

- Is perceptive about themselves, deploying their own strengths, facing up to their weaknesses, and finding ways to manage them instead of just denying or ignoring them
- Pays attention to developing their emotional competence in relating to others and can appreciate and resolve interpersonal difficulties
- Understands how using psychometric tools can assist this process, as they provide a powerful source for self-development, including knowing their bias towards:
  - Extraversion or Introversion
  - Thinking or Feeling
  - Sensing or Intuition

  and the impact this has on others
- Knows that, by developing their understanding of self and others, they get a better insight into the work most suitable for them, for dealing with people they find more difficult to get on with, for discovering dormant talents they may have and for developing their own sense of self-leadership

Part 2: The Mindset

The Pioneer:

- Is not a Work Victim! They create their own success, and rather than waiting for a perfect world, they take responsibility for shaping and managing their own environment well.

- Keeps their skills current, knowing that they can't expect other people to invest in them if they don't invest in themselves. They operate a business within a business, realising no one cares as much about their own success as they do.

- Works Interdependently, co-operating well with other people from a platform of self-worth, they take others' needs into account.

- Has The Mindset of Responsible Initiative; they present solutions not problems, they take responsibility for creating their own success and ask, 'If this were my company, what would I do?'

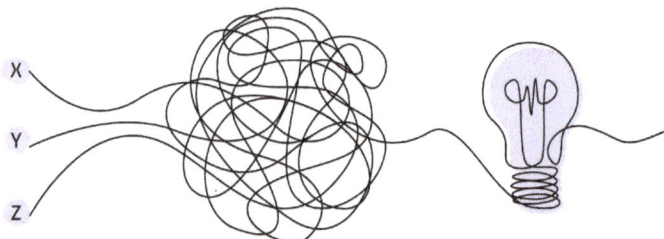

THE STEPS

Three Critical Steps
Step One: Preparing
Step Two: Positioning
Step Three: Performing
In a nutshell
Chapter summary

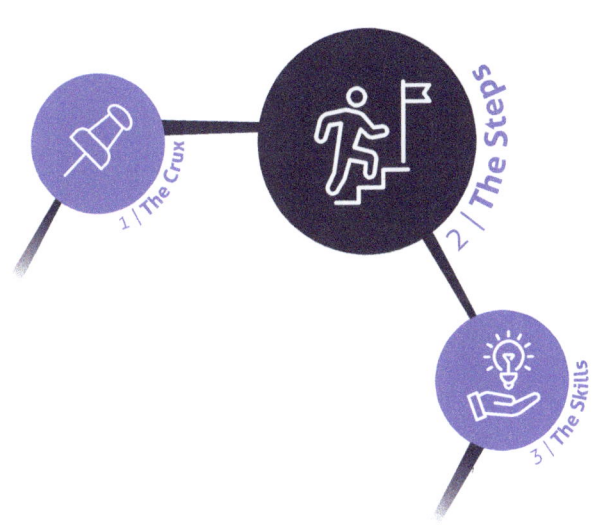

'You are braver than you believe, stronger than you seem, and smarter than you think.'
— A A Milne

Three Critical Steps

Understanding the Three Critical Steps that Pioneers adopt to achieve success will help you to get going, with the best chance of success.

As with all crafts, hobbies, and indeed when you learn new skills or languages, there are things you need to know, tools you need to acquire, and practice you need to go through, before you become proficient. It is the same for learning The Skills of The Pioneer.

When we learn new skills, we go through a model of unconscious incompetence, to unconscious competence which is always the goal. Many never achieve the success they would like because they don't do the work needed to get to the level of unconscious competence.

If you can think of something you have had to learn like a foreign language, taking up a new musical instrument or perhaps learning to ride a bike or drive a car, these are the learning stages we go through:

- **Unconscious Incompetence:** we don't know what we don't know, we are oblivious to this discipline/language/skill.

- **Conscious Incompetence:** we become aware of the language we need to learn or we see another child riding a bicycle, and we start to investigate. Maybe we enrol in an online programme to learn the language, or our parents give us a bicycle and we get started. This is the stage of curiosity and perhaps excitement or worry: now that we know, do we have the time and aptitude to learn this thing?

- **Conscious Competence:** we are actively learning – we hesitantly start speaking in the language to practise, we go out on our bicycle with an adult, running along with us, holding the back of the seat. This stage can take quite a while, depending on the amount of practice we put in. It can get hard. I can think of people who have decided to learn a musical instrument. In the beginning, it's exciting and it doesn't matter what the notes sound like in the early stages. But now at this stage of active learning, it is the tedious practice you have to put in that matters. The early excitement has worn off and it's hard to keep going. Sometimes it feels as if you are not progressing at all, and many give up at this stage. It's hard.

- **Unconscious Competence:** the stage of excellence. We have put in the practice, we have done the work, and now we can ride the bicycle expertly on our own, we can speak the language fluently, we can play the instrument like a maestro, without even thinking about it. Others might say 'You are lucky' or 'You are talented'... but you know it has taken a lot of hard work and sheer determination.

With the Three Critical Steps, we hope to get you going fast to the Unconscious Competence stage, as a Pioneer of your own career and life.

> 'The most difficult thing is to act,
> the rest is merely tenacity.'
> — Amelia Earhart

So, the Three Critical Steps are Preparing, Positioning and Performing. In this chapter, we will give you an overview of each one in turn, and a quick peek at The Skills which flow through The Steps. Then, in the chapters which follow, we will help you understand and apply them all.

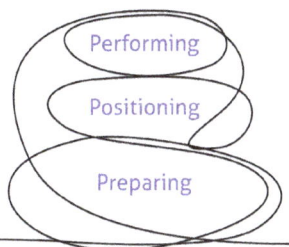

Step One: Preparing

They say that with most projects, 90% is preparation, 10% is execution or decoration.

THE PIONEER

I certainly know from making celebration cakes that 90% of my time is spent deciding on my design and how I'm going to do it, gathering my tools, making the cakes, shaping the cakes, sticking them together, and applying the foundation icing. When all of that is done, then I can do the fancy design, which takes little time in comparison. It would be stressful doing the decoration without this solid foundation and knowing where I was heading and what I needed.

The Preparing Step for The Pioneer is like that too. Put in the work here to really ground yourself, and build your sense of self-worth and appreciation. When you have done that, you can work on your understanding and appreciation of others.

There are 7 Key Skills which the Pioneers in our research had, which set them apart from the rest. The first, and the most important skill at this Step, is called: *Develops Personal Excellence*. In the next chapter, we take you deeper into this skill and the attitudes and principles which lead to Personal Excellence. This is the hard bit, which requires you to purposefully shape your environment and develop your own Personal Power. It is the needed preparation for The Skills which follow. Developing Personal Excellence needs practice and dedication to master. When you do, the results will be clear for everyone to see.

With your Preparation done, you are now ready to Position yourself for success.

Step Two: Positioning

This Step, covered in Chapter 4, The Secrets, is all about building the skills needed for you to be able to perform well. Some of them may be strengths of yours already, some may need a little brush-up. Knowing what they are and the action you need to take is therefore vital. Treat it like a little health check. We keep our cars and machines well-oiled and serviced, but rarely do we give ourselves this level of care and attention.

Our experience is the three Skills at this Step are not often thought about or worked on, so much so we call them The Secrets. They are: *Seeks Clarity, Negotiates for Success*, and *Builds Strategic Business Acumen*.

Chapter 4 takes you deeply into each one of these skills, so you are supported all the way. This means you can work on The Skills and Position yourself well for what follows.

Seeks Clarity is about questioning until you are clear about what you need to do, why you need to do it and how, rather than going off on a wrong course of action. Maybe you are wary of asking too many questions from bad experiences in the past, or the particular style of the leader. Understanding this skill will give you a kit bag of different questioning techniques, to get you through each situation. The way you go about this is important, and, curiously, as you get skilled at questioning, you also need to listen. The two go hand in hand. You can't have good questioning without also building your Effective Listening skills.

Then you work on *Negotiating for Success*. Pioneers are great negotiators who always strive for win-win outcomes for all parties involved, wherever possible. This book will help you to understand your natural bias in terms of negotiating, what might be holding you back and what you can do about it.

Paying attention then to *Building Strategic Business Acumen* is key. It is all too easy to get busy, daily, with the operational and tactical parts of your role. You know what you need to do and when. This skill is all about seeing above the parapet, knowing how what you are doing fits in with the strategic goals of the organisation and why your job matters, and this book will help you with developing in this area.

Part of thinking strategically is about managing your manager well, which people often fail to appreciate they have any control over. By focusing your attention, you will find you have more control and impact than you think.

Now you are Positioned well to Perform at a higher level and take on the next set of Skills. Chunking them step by step like this, hopefully helps you. You can make one change at a time, to move you to the Unconscious Competence level much more easily.

Step Three: Performing

This is where you really start to flex your wings, broaden your style and wake up to the fact that no one cares as much about your development as you do. If you want to be more and do more, there is no one holding you back except you. You are in control of your destiny, of your outlook on life, of your inner peace and happiness, of your success.

The three Skills needed at this stage are: *Controls Own Workload*, *Manages Own Learning* and *Takes Charge of Own Career*.

Many people we speak to are good citizens; they work hard and are courteous to others, but seldom do they display outstanding levels of performance. There is always so much to do, an endless list of tasks to get through. 'I could be amazing if only I could get through this lot,' is often the thought process. And time slips by. You notice you have somehow reached the next decade without realising your true potential or achieving the success you desire.

This Skill of *Controls Own Workload* is needed right now at this stage to help you Perform at a higher level for you.

> 'If a man is called to be a street sweeper, he should sweep streets even as a Michaelangelo painted, or Beethoven composed music or

> Shakespeare wrote poetry. He should sweep streets so well that all the hosts of heaven and earth will pause to say, "Here lived a great street sweeper who did his job well."
> — Dr Martin Luther King Jr

This is about lifting your sights higher, Performing your job better than ever before. This comes through constant daily practice, and it is here, where you are managing your workload well, that change can happen.

Controls Own Workload involves managing not only your work projects and understanding the blockers that get in your way, but it also involves defining your Achilles Heel. This is the niggly thing that trips you over every time. Working on a plan to overcome it is critical.

Moving onto the next Skill at this Step, *Manages Own Learning*, this is where you realise that not everything is going to be handed to you on a plate. If you want to go on a training course, you need to ask for it rather than waiting for it to be offered to you. If you would like a different role or more responsibility, you make it known and act as if you are already doing that role.

You understand learning as a cycle and are alert to becoming stuck in that cycle, and you avoid going there. You know that you learn far more from making mistakes than by doing things perfectly, so you treat mistakes as learning opportunities and become skilled in handling them. You understand how to give and receive feedback well, and you know exactly what action to take.

This leads nicely into the seventh of the 7 Key Skills, which is *Takes Charge of Own Career*. Having done all the Preparation on yourself and having Positioned yourself well, you are now in a good state to chart your own career and make the most of the gifts you have. Having a keen understanding of what motivates and drives you and how this differs from others, allows you to proactively manage your own business. This is where you operate yourself like a PLC, knowing what your stakeholders, shareholders, staff, systems and suppliers need, and you write your three-year plan. Your plan is created by you, driven by you, Inspired by you, for you, and it charts your course for greater success.

You may have come across some or all of these Skills before. Viewing them as a process, a series of Steps, helps you to achieve success faster than you might have done otherwise. And rigorously building The Skills as the Pioneers in our research did, was what set them apart from the rest, and gave them greater success, peace and balance in their lives.

In a nutshell

Before we dive properly into The Skills, let's take stock – we have covered quite a lot of ground so far. This is how things come together.

The Crux

The Mirror: Understands self and others

By managing relationships well, you understand individual differences, including among your customers, colleagues and managers; you make the best use of your own and others' strengths.

The Mindset: Responsible Initiative

Presenting solutions not problems; you see a problem and take responsibility for ensuring it is dealt with; you have a hassle-free, self-directing approach to managing self, others and life.

The Steps

Step One: Preparing

Skill 1: Develops Personal Excellence: Shaping your own environment, by developing your own Personal Power and sense of assertion and balance; developing your Emotional Intelligence (EQ) to handle yourself and others well.

Step Two: Positioning

Skill 2: Seeks Clarity – why, what and how? Using a range of powerful questioning techniques and actively listening to explore what is required of you, to reduce ambiguity, establish a clear brief and determine expectations.

Skill 3: Negotiates for Success: Understanding your own bias towards influencing, negotiating and conflict resolution; being skilled in the use of a Powerful Negotiation Strategy to achieve win-win outcomes for all.

Skill 4: Builds Strategic Business Acumen: Thinking skilfully and strategically, as well as tactically and operationally. You have nous and actively manage your manager; you expertly solve problems and appreciate the culture you are working in.

Step Three: Performing

Skill 5: Controls Own Workload: Being in control of your workload profile by recognising and managing known behavioural traits which can trip you up; you manage stress well and are acutely aware of your own Achilles Heel, taking action to counter it.

Skill 6: Manages Own Learning: Investing in your own business as a way of life, knowing that learning is a cycle of change. You treat mistakes as learning opportunities and understand the importance of seeking and receiving feedback while knowing the parameters for success.

Skill 7: Takes Charge of Own Career: Creatively self-reliant, you know your own motivations and manage your own business well by writing your career plan, like a business plan – Me PLC. You use powerful networking skills and constantly adapt to change.

The self-directing approach of The Pioneer comes together in a cohesive wheel, like this:

The Pioneer Wheel

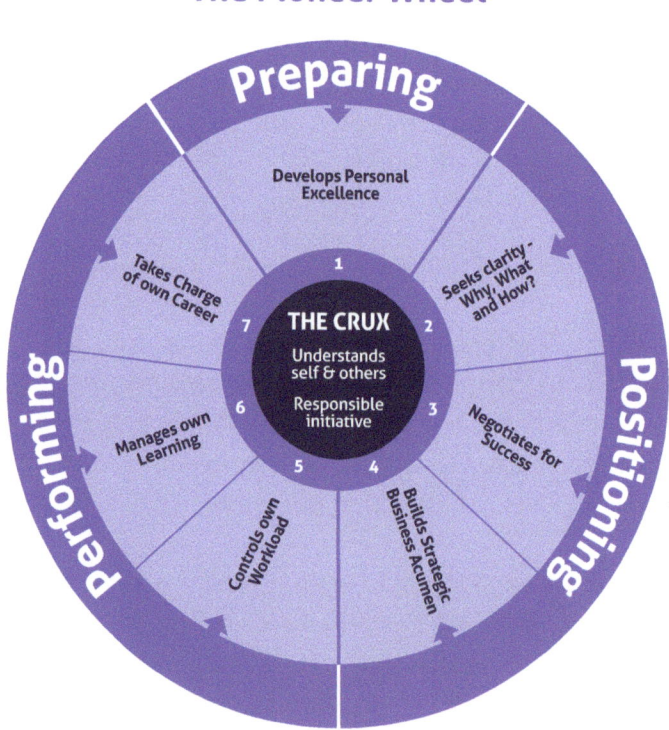

Case study: Julian, the Work Victim – revisited

Julian had not assumed The Mindset of The Pioneer. Although he was an optimistic person and very willing, his assumptions were based more on being led within an organisation which, even if not perfect, would go a long way towards providing the means for his own rapid success. He had not expected the frantic business and seeming chaos of today's modern organisations, and that within this he had to shape his own environment for success.

If Julian changes his approach, there is much he can do to regain control over his own destiny and success. He can ensure that, by asking the right questions, he can get clear project briefs, including exploring some of the nuances involved, instead of passively taking instructions. If he's not getting the feedback to help him learn rapidly, he can ask his manager for it, and handle the interaction so that it is timely and rewarding both for him and his manager. He can work with clients on a basis of understanding their needs so as to meet them, rather than promoting his own technical expertise. He can take control of his own workflow instead of just being carried along by it.

All this, of course, requires a different approach from the initial one which Julian adopted, and where he ended up as a Work Victim. A self-directing approach would be much more profitable for Julian and, if this is carried through with The Skills associated with it, it would position him to get a lot more of what he wants.

These Skills mean:

- Developing a clear knowledge of your own and others' strengths and weaknesses and understanding how to use your abilities to maximum effect

- Taking personal responsibility for creating the conditions you need to succeed, and if you are unclear about what is required, you proactively and skilfully question your manager and clients to get a clear brief

- Negotiating positively to get the best possible result, managing conflicting priorities well, and adding value with suggestions and ideas for improvement

- Having considerable savvy. You have a solid understanding of commercial needs and priorities and are keenly aware of the wider implications of the actions you take

- Taking control of your workload, keeping track of your commitments and using Positive Negotiation to establish priorities, you reliably deliver on the actions you have promised

- Creating your own learning opportunities, such as seeking feedback and handling mistakes in a mature fashion, adding to your credibility

- Confidently using your initiative in unclear or risky areas but also being aware of when you need help and are not afraid to ask for it

- Developing an understanding of the organisation you work for and the way things are done there; you are sensitive to the needs of the organisation and others and know that success comes from building networks based on good long-term relationships

Chapter summary

The Pioneer:

- Understands the need to move through the levels to unconscious competence when learning new skills. They know it takes consistent daily practice until success and balance seem effortless.

- Appreciates there are Three Critical Steps to guide them on their way:

    — Step One: Preparing

    — Step Two: Positioning

    — Step Three: Performing

- Clearly sees the 7 Key Skills flowing through the Steps, and proactively and consistently works to develop these:

- Preparing:

    Skill 1: Develops Personal Excellence

- Positioning:

    Skill 2: Seeks Clarity – why, what and how?

    Skill 3: Negotiates for Success

    Skill 4: Builds Strategic Business Acumen

- Performing:

    Skill 5: Controls Own Workload

    Skill 6: Manages Own Learning

    Skill 7: Takes Charge of Own Career

- Knows how important it is to start at the beginning by developing their own sense of self, really getting to the root of what drives them and others. They develop their Responsible Initiative through the full range of Skills identified.

THE SKILLS: PREPARING FOR INCREASED PERSONAL EXCELLENCE

Skill 1: Develops Personal Excellence
Changes in the work environment
Personal Power
Removing self-imposed barriers
Emotional Intelligence
Underpinning attitudes
Chapter summary

'You don't have to be confined by your environment, by your family or circumstances, and certainly not by your race or gender.'
— Mariah Carey

Skill 1: Develops Personal Excellence

> Shaping your own environment by developing your own Personal Power and sense of assertion and balance; developing your Emotional Intelligence (EQ) to handle yourself and others well.

We live in a constantly changing world, and Pioneers are adept at responding positively to change. It is always lovely to reminisce about the 'old days', and how things were 'back then', but we need to learn to do this without getting stuck there, without putting up barriers and obstructing change. The skill is to move on resolutely with commitment and passion.

This is sometimes easier to do than at other times, depending on the change being experienced, which could be personal to you, or organisation-wide or global. Seeking the help you need and moving on is key, and so too is understanding how things have changed over time.

Changes in the work environment

The work environment has changed considerably over recent years making The Pioneer approach more important than ever. Such changes include:

- **Empowerment:** Where greater responsibility is passed 'down the line', requiring people to take more ownership and Responsible Initiative in identifying what needs to be done, and then taking appropriate action.

- **Increased span of control/delayering:** This usually results in there being fewer managers and therefore less available time with those who remain.

- **Service orientation:** The emphasis now is on meeting clients' expectations and needs and building productive relationships with them. Technical expertise and knowledge by themselves are no longer enough, and in fact, is just the starting point.

- **Increased performance expectations:** Today's organisations have little room for coasting or mediocre performance. 'Enough to get by' is simply not enough, especially when it comes to managing your own career.

- **Constant change:** The changing world of work requires continuous learning, a curiosity

SKILL 1: DEVELOPS PERSONAL EXCELLENCE

to explore and keep developing new skills, knowledge and interests.

- **Workforce flexibility:** This means being able to do many things well and adjusting to constantly changing circumstances.

- **Remote working:** The ability to work away from the office requires greater reliance on self-management, self-direction and motivation if you are to continuously give your best and excel, wherever you are.

Many Work Victims don't cope well with such changes and revert to playing the 'ain't it awful' game, blaming others, society, the organisation, their manager, their situation, whatever. They use their energy to reinforce their feeling of powerlessness. Others are realistic about the reality of change and harness their energy to manage their situation and environment within these realities. They concentrate on the considerable amount they can influence.

It often happens that many of the restraints people put on themselves are self-imposed, and stem from the frame of mind or attitude with which they perceive the situation. For example, let's imagine two people experiencing the same difficult work situation; one's view might be:

> 'Life is a rat race. I'm always trying to catch up, meet deadlines which aren't important but are just routine. So even though I'm nervous and tense, I'm also bored a lot of the time.'

The other person says:

> 'I'm almost never bored. Even when there's something I have to do that doesn't strike me as interesting at first, I usually find it worthwhile in a way that teaches me something and enables me to shape a future and productive work life for myself.'

As a test of how you see your general situation, ask yourself the question 'How can I succeed when…?', then list the things that are getting in your way in the box or in a notepad:

SKILL 1: DEVELOPS PERSONAL EXCELLENCE

Be honest with yourself.

When you review your responses again later, you may view them differently, as problems or restraints, rather than givens.

In other words, you have a choice!

Personal Power

Power carries many negative connotations, and has been abused countless times throughout history due to its potential to do harm or to oppress. Yet power is the mainspring of making positive things happen too, which benefit all. Without a power source, little is likely to be achieved, for good or ill. Powerlessness, the feeling of having no control over events or choices, is a state which generates much stress, anxiety and mental anguish, as well as creating low self-esteem.

Within organisations, there are many sources of power: position power, role power, power based on knowledge, information, money or charisma. Sometimes, and maybe more outside work, physical and sometimes sexual power can be added to the mix.

The Pioneer has access to a large source of power. This is Personal Power, carried within themselves. Personal Power differs from other forms of power because it is based on the individual, not the role, 'uniform' or organisation. It comes from using The Skills with Responsible

Initiative. It is founded on both a state of mind and a set of Skills, to follow things through. This 'can-do' attitude carries through to successful completion, using the tools to make the right things happen. Of course, The Mindset and Skills feed upon themselves – an increase in one results in a corresponding increase in the other.

The Pioneer is not powerless, rather they use their Personal Power to manage their own environment towards a better outcome. Most people have much more Personal Power than they realise. They just need to get in touch with it, that's all, and use it through some of the focused skills we shall be exploring shortly. They create *Em*powerment as opposed to *Dis*empowerment.

In today's organisational world, Personal Power is replacing the 'command and control' hierarchical-based power that managers traditionally exercised. The additional bonus of getting in touch with and exercising your Personal Power is how it can improve the richness of life generally.

> **TOP TIP**
>
> Today, success hinges on the ability to influence people to achieve common goals and purposes. This power to influence is personal effectiveness. It is the new power of competence. Such power is based on the person, not their position.
>
> It is... **Personal Power**.

Removing self-imposed barriers

Another way of seeing what The Pioneer is all about is in the way they approach many of the restraints we can put on ourselves. It is worth looking, in a new light, at the points made earlier about our perfect setting.

Perfect manager: Waiting for the perfect manager to come along to allow you to grow to your full potential is like waiting for a lottery win. Sometimes your manager will be good, other times less so. Instead of just being a passive respondent in the situation, self-directing people use their skills to manage their manager. They do this by asking themselves questions like:

- What does my manager want?
- What annoys my manager?
- What makes my manager feel positive?
- What is it that my manager really appreciates?

This is not a take-over bid, but simply a way of recognising and harnessing your manager's strengths and finding ways to cope with their weaknesses so you can achieve the best possible job, and accomplish what you need.

There will be an opportunity for you to think about and answer the above questions in Chapter 4.

Perfect organisation: The Pioneer makes the best use of the environment they are in. They decide what is important, rather than trying to 'slay every dragon', and shape their own environment to get it:

- Not getting feedback? *Ask for it.*
- Swamped with inappropriate work? *Negotiate priorities.*
- Interrupted every five minutes so you can't get on with things? *Create disturb and don't disturb zones.*
- Want to flex your wings and try out your management ability? *Ask to lead a project.*

Perfect colleagues: It matters to you that you do a successful job, on time, but this is dependent on others, and somehow there is always a problem, and you get the blame for poor delivery. The Pioneer does not accept this, neither do they whinge about it. They anticipate the problem, work out what needs to be done, make positive suggestions to their manager and take responsibility for implementing what is agreed.

Perfect clients: The client seems to respect your expertise but somehow you end up jumping through hoops because they don't seem to know what they want, and the job ends up satisfying no one completely, including yourself. The Pioneer takes responsibility for clearly establishing at the outset what the client wants so they can deliver well. They also proactively build up good, productive relationships with them which develop into strategic partnerships. They see the world from the client's perspective, not just from their own technical specialism.

Perfect you: Sad to say, you are unlikely to be perfect. You will have strengths and corresponding weaknesses, and knowing and recognising them helps. The good news is that you can be better, which is what the quest of The Pioneer is all about. They take responsibility for their own continuous learning and improvement.

Also, we may have 'booby-trapped' ourselves by carrying around assumptions or 'life scripts' from the past. It is useful to review these and test them out by revisiting the question 'How can I succeed when…?'

Are these constraints self-imposed or real? How do other people deal with them?

Emotional Intelligence

In recent years, a stream of research has emerged on Emotional Intelligence (Daniel Goleman's work[3]) which has had a striking impact on management thinking and practice.

The thinking is that there are three domains of excellence:

---
3   Goleman, D, *Emotional Intelligence* (Bantam Books, 2006)

- **Intellectual:** as supposedly measured by IQ
- **Expertise:** practical intelligence, technical expertise and experience
- **Emotional:** emotional and interpersonal intelligence

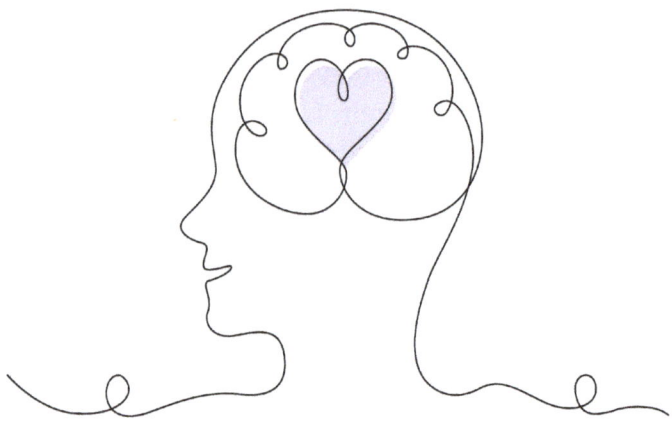

There are relationships between these three. For example, Emotional Intelligence skills do have a connection with intellectual ones. Top performers have both. The aptitude for success starts with intellectual horsepower, but people need Emotional Competence too, if they are to release the full potential of their talent.

In today's world, Expertise is seen to be a baseline competence needed to get the job done. However, in addition to Expertise, how the job is done through the Emotional Intelligence competencies, determines performance. It is about being able to translate Expertise into something relevant and useful. For example, while one computer programmer relates only to their own 'techy expertise', another more successful one will be additionally skilled in relating to their client's needs.

Emotional Intelligence is not the same as Emotional Competence. Competence is the learned application of this form of intelligence. What comes out of the research, clearly, is that it is Emotional Competence skills, underpinned by baseline Expertise, which lead to excellence and superior performance. The nature of what is required depends on the particular job: the more senior it is, the more these skills are likely to be required, but even at a junior level they make a significant difference.

It is no wonder, then, that modern recruitment practice establishes, and takes for granted, academic, intellectual and technical ability, and also looks for personal qualities – eg the initiative and adaptability of Emotional Competence.

There is a clear, supporting, correlation between The Mindset and the 7 Key Skills of The Pioneer and Emotional Competence. The 7 Key Skills are generic ones, applicable along the spectrum of Emotional Intelligence.

The research we conducted demonstrated that the 'value added' of people with high Emotional Competence for different types of roles was:

- Low-complexity jobs, eg operators, clerks: The top 1% was three times more productive than the bottom 1%

- Medium-complexity jobs, eg sales clerks, mechanics: The top 1% was twelve times more productive than the bottom 1%

- High-complexity jobs, eg insurance salespeople, account managers, lawyers, doctors: The top 1% was 2.3 times more productive than average-ranking performers

Emotional Intelligence is not about:

- Being nice, but being real and genuine

- Shooting from the hip, but managing feelings and expressing them appropriately

- Gender stereotypes, but recognising that all people have strengths and weaknesses

- Having a fixed aptitude, but about development over a lifetime

The Emotional Intelligence qualities identified in Daniel Goleman's research (*Working With Emotional Intelligence*[4]) are shown below. Some are innate qualities while others need to be developed from potential to competence through training and application. If they appear intimidating in their comprehensiveness, remember that not all jobs require the full range, and

---

4   Goleman, D, *Working With Emotional Intelligence* (Bloomsbury Publishing, 1999)

SKILL 1: DEVELOPS PERSONAL EXCELLENCE

that the 7 Key Skills provide a solid foundation for enhancing professional excellence.

Personal Competence *How we manage ourselves*	Social Competence *How we handle relationships*
Self-awareness - *knowing own preferences and intuitions* • Emotional awareness • Accurate self-assessment • Self-confidence Self-regulation - *managing own internal states and impulses* • Self-control • Trustworthiness • Conscientiousness • Adaptability • Innovation Motivation - *emotional tendencies that guide us to reach our goals* • Achievement drive • Commitment • Initiative • Optimism	Empathy - *awareness of others' feelings, needs and concerns* • Understanding others • Developing others • Service orientation • Leveraging diversity • Political awareness Social skills - *skill at inducing desirable responses in others* • Influence • Communication • Conflict management • Leadership • Change catalyst • Building bonds • Collaboration and co-operation • Team capabilities

Underpinning attitudes

Another perspective on the self-directing frame of mind comes from the OK Corral model, which is derived from the theories of Transactional Analysis. It is a useful tool when you need to understand why an individual is responding to you in a particular way, and what attitude you need to adopt to best handle the situation.

From an early age, people develop a view of their own worth and tend to take 'life positions' relative to other people. Life positions develop from experiences, particularly those during childhood, and affect the way people feel, act and relate to others.

The OK Corral model is concerned with two basic views, which an individual will have in mind when dealing with another person.

Firstly, how I view myself:

- **I'm OK:** My self-esteem is reasonably high, I feel comfortable with this environment, and I feel able to cope.
- **I'm not OK:** I'm uncomfortable dealing with this sort of issue, I don't feel I have the necessary skills.

While I am sorting out my own underlying attitude towards me, I am also viewing you, the other person. I am dealing with you in one of two ways:

- **You're OK:** You have a right to your opinions. You are essentially decent. You have a contribution to make.
- **You're not OK:** You never listen. You are wrong. You won't win this one.

The combination of my view of me and my view of you gives the possibility of four positions, or attitudes, as shown in the diagram. Each position is typified by particular types of behaviour.

SKILL 1: DEVELOPS PERSONAL EXCELLENCE

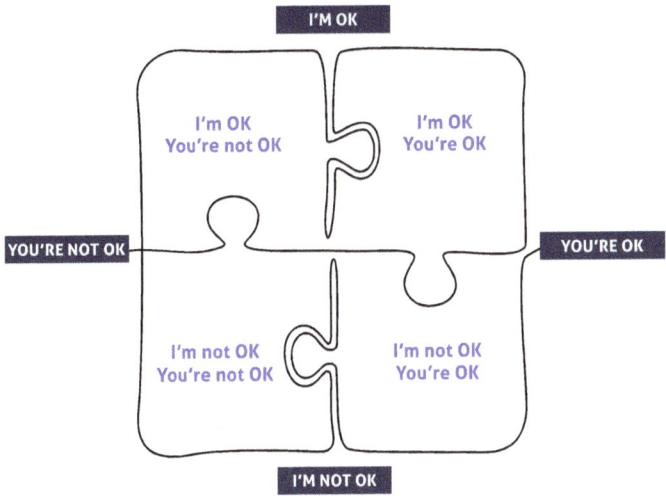

I+U- (I'm OK, You're not OK). If this is your underlying attitude, then your behaviour will indicate a feeling of superiority, either through an aggressive stance or an over-protective parental approach. This is likely to provoke resistance, aggression or dependence from the other party.

I-U- (I'm not OK, You're not OK). This attitude is commonly held by those experiencing change. It manifests itself in a suspicious and often hostile approach to others with an underlying feeling of 'Why bother? It won't make any difference anyway.' To be on the receiving end of this type of behaviour can be frustrating and exhausting and requires considerable effort to deal with it appropriately.

I-U+ (I'm not OK, You're OK). If you're viewing life from this position, it's likely that your self-esteem has taken a knock. You are susceptible to being rescued by the other person who is OK in your mind. Behaviour emanating from this position is non-assertive and often yielding, which in turn can lead to a further dip in your self-esteem. An interesting factor about those who often inhabit this quadrant is the lightning switch they can make to I+U-. When the final straw is delivered, the method of dealing with it is often an extremely aggressive approach which surprises all parties.

I+U+ (I'm OK, You're OK). This is the most productive position to occupy, whenever possible. Behaviours are assertive and warm, and the underlying attitude is one of Positive Regard and trust, even when delivering bad news or having a potentially unpleasant conversation. Your expectations of the other person are consistently high. When expectations are high, the chances of those expectations being met are significantly increased. Being on the receiving end of I+U+ behaviours is irresistible. In time, the other party will join you in that quadrant.

How basic attitude influences behaviour

Identify where you (and your colleagues) stand in the following matrix:

How people behave when their basic attitude is:	I'm OK You're not OK	I'm not OK You're not OK	I'm not OK You're OK	I'm OK You're OK
Communicates	Defensively Aggressively	With hostility Abruptly	Defensively Aggressively	Openly
Handles disagreements	By placing the blame on others	By escalating the conflict and involving a third party	By perceiving differences as evidence of inadequacy	By seeking clarification and mutual resolution
Solves problems	By unilaterally rejecting others' ideas and looking for win:lose positions	By giving in to the problem	By relying almost completely on others	By consulting others and trusting self
Gives feedback	Harshly, by attaching the blame to the participant	Half-heartedly, by disowning the feedback and blaming the process	Hesitatingly and with no clarity	Assertively, tactfully and explicitly
Accepts feedback	Argumentatively, challenging every point	Passively, unwillingly, looking to blame others	Timidly and unquestioningly	Readily and with gratitude, and takes action
Feels to others	Superior	Alienated	Inferior	Equal

In terms of the OK Corral model, the approach of The Pioneer aligns most closely with the I+U+ quadrant. But this isn't the end of the story. People who are Independent, rather than truly Interdependent, may operate in an I+U+ fashion in that they engage with other people's needs, but they do not do so in a way which achieves the most productive results.

This is particularly so when there are difficulties in the relationship. Remember the set of characteristics of Responsible Initiative include:

- Taking others' needs into account (this does not mean slavishly following them)
- Taking the longer view, by working to make the project, unit or company a success rather than just concentrating on your own work

What often makes the difference between the Independent I+U+ and the Interdependent I+U+ are two distinct characteristics called Positive Regard and Genuineness.

Coming from good counselling theory, research shows clearly that effective counsellors need to have these two characteristics before they can help their clients. If they don't display these characteristics, then their clients won't respond to them. These findings are extremely relevant to the way in which The Pioneer behaves, especially in relation to helping to improve another's job performance.

SKILL 1: DEVELOPS PERSONAL EXCELLENCE

The two characteristics are:

Positive Regard	Genuineness
This means having respect for the other person as an individual and a positive belief in them as a person. Irrespective of the behaviour they are displaying, you see the good in them and view them as a decent human being.	This means that you are able to express your own feelings and tell the truth about your reaction to another person's behaviour. It means being direct, open and honest with the other person, not shying away from difficult conversations.

Without these underlying characteristics or attitudes, you are unlikely to persuade the other person to change and enhance their performance. Also, without them, the interaction is likely to be experienced as false, patronising or manipulative. With them, however, not only is the process destined to go well, but the interaction does not have to be technically perfect in order to be a success. In other words:

- The underlying attitudes of Positive Regard and Genuineness are even more important than the skills of conducting the discussion
- Without them, you will have little real influence on other people, particularly those whose performance you wish to help to improve significantly

Maintaining Positive Regard

It is not always easy to maintain Positive Regard. In situations where such a difficulty can be anticipated, it is useful to prepare by thinking about the other person in the following ways:

- Identify some of their strengths, not just their weaknesses.
- Develop a vision of them performing at their best.
- Remember that everyone has reasons for behaving the way they do.
- Think back to a time when you felt good about them.

Be tough with the individual if necessary, but do so out of Positive Regard. In difficult circumstances, it may pay you to confront the other person with your feelings about what they are doing. This is part of being Genuine.

Being Genuine

As well as having Positive Regard for their clients, research has shown clearly that effective counsellors also have a high degree of Genuineness. Genuineness means expressing your own feelings and telling the truth about your reaction to the behaviour of the other person. It means being direct, open and honest.

Again, this is common sense. It is better to engage with the other person directly, as a human being, and not hide behind a façade of being the perfect manager,

SKILL 1: DEVELOPS PERSONAL EXCELLENCE

always in control, measured and dispassionate. It is about being straight with the other person.

Clearly, this does not mean losing your temper or over-reacting. Rather, it is concerned with having sufficient Positive Regard for the other person to 'tell it like it is', concentrating on what they do (the behaviour) that is causing good or poor performance. Remember, Positive Regard values the person as a person, but it does not necessarily value their behaviour.

Confronting someone in this way is a particularly powerful way to get them to change and improve their performance. For example:

> 'Matt, I feel angry and sad that I just can't rely on your work. Every time I give you a job to do, you do it willingly and turn it around quickly. I really appreciate that. But what gets me is that there are always silly mistakes in your work. They spoil a good job and it's a shame. What makes me most angry is that I've raised this with you before, several times, and you haven't done anything about it. So, come on Matt, sort this out, I know you can do it. Check your work before you pass it on to me and you'll be doing a great job.'

If you keep your feelings bottled up, they will leak out anyway through body language and may be misinterpreted. Alternatively, they will come out at a later stage with irritation or anger. Also, if the interaction is not open and honest or – worse still – is manipulative, then the other person will soon sense this. You can rarely keep feelings as hidden as you think you can!

Genuineness and Positive Regard are complementary, and it is not possible to have Positive Regard without being Genuine. Both are essential attitudes for feedback, for effective performance reviews and for improvement to take place. Also, applying these attitudes well requires you to be appropriately assertive, as you will see from the next table.

Only by being assertive, rather than too aggressive or non-assertive can you achieve the desired win-win outcomes for all.

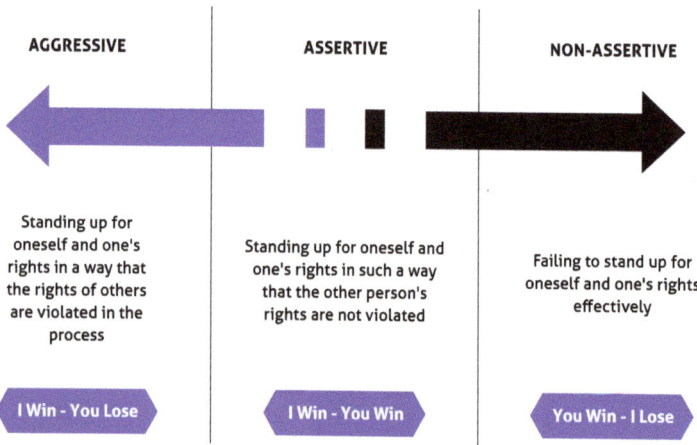

SKILL 1: DEVELOPS PERSONAL EXCELLENCE

Some people, depending on their personality type, may confuse assertion with aggression, which it most certainly is not. Assertion is a way of being, where you stand up for yourself and listen to and validate the other person's view. Assertion is very much part of your standing in your Personal Power.

Chapter summary

The Pioneer:

- Is adept at harnessing their own Personal Excellence, by working on their attitudes and behaviours to continually develop

- Adapts well to changes in their work environment, appreciating they have a choice in the way they respond, viewing life as an exciting adventure

- Appreciates they have access to a large source of power, Personal Power, carried within themselves. This means, irrespective of their level in the organisation, their 'can-do' attitude carries through to making the right things happen

- Knows how to get around self-imposed barriers and take action in a less-than-perfect world, tapping into their Emotional Intelligence to add value

- Understands how to communicate with the right state of mind – I'm OK, You're OK – taking others' needs into account, and taking a longer-term view
- Uses the attitudes of Positive Regard and Genuineness to help them effect truly Interdependent behaviour
- Is appropriately assertive, standing up for their own needs while respecting those of the other person, ensuring win-win outcomes for all

THE SECRETS: POSITIONING YOURSELF WELL FOR SUCCESS

Skill 2: Seeks Clarity – why, what and how?
Questioning using Responsible Initiative
Active and Effective Listening
Effective Questioning
Putting Open and Closed Questions to work
Gaining Quality Information

Skill 3: Negotiates for Success
Positive Negotiation and conflict management
Negotiation styles
Conflict resolution
Powerful Negotiation Strategy

Skill 4: Builds Strategic Business Acumen
What is Strategic Business Acumen?
How to manage your manager
Tackling problems and opportunities with Responsible Initiative
Organisation culture
Chapter summary

'Believe you can and you're halfway there.'
— Theodore Roosevelt

Skill 2: Seeks Clarity – why, what and how?

> Using a range of powerful questioning techniques and actively listening to explore what is required of you, to reduce ambiguity, establish a clear brief and determine expectations.

In terms of The Pioneer's 6-Point Plan, these next three positioning skills are called The Secrets. This is because they are hidden in plain sight. We all know about questioning, listening and negotiating, although may be less familiar with thinking strategically. However, all these skills are probably in the background of your thoughts.

By shining a light on them here, it gives you a chance to review them, so you can consciously build your competence in them. We continue now with Skill 2, where you question to seek clarity by asking why, what and how?

Questioning using Responsible Initiative

It is astonishing and sad how Dependent people miss out on so many opportunities for richness in their personal lives and in the workplace. They put themselves in a powerless, 'can't do' situation because they rely on 'they', whoever 'they' are, to provide them with important information and direction. It is as if they need to be continuously spoon-fed information or the help they need.

People who use initiative irresponsibly aren't bothered by information: they work on the fallacy that they have somehow guessed correctly the information they need. The Pioneer knows when to proactively obtain information. They know that the solution to many of their issues is to *ask*.

It used to be said that 'those who ask, don't get'. This was an admonition used frequently in childhood. Yet, in adulthood at least, the reverse is true: those who don't ask, don't get, while those who ask often do.

For example:

- If your manager or a client isn't being clear about what they want: *Ask, appropriately, until you have a clear mental picture of what is wanted.*

- If you don't have the background information to do your work well: *Ask for it.*

SKILL 2: SEEKS CLARITY – WHY, WHAT AND HOW?

- If you are not getting the feedback or help to learn a new skill quickly: *Ask for it.*
- If you want to attend a training programme, but you haven't been invited yet: *Ask to attend.*

So, what's the big deal? Everyone uses Questioning and Listening, don't they? Surely they have been doing it all their lives?

> **TOP TIP**
>
> Taking Responsible Initiative is The Mindset needed for Personal Excellence and success. Likewise, Questioning and Listening when used with Responsible Initiative, are the most important Skills and form the bedrock for The Skills which follow.

The Pioneer has learned some refined Questioning skills, which enables them to obtain Quality Information quickly and well, to hear and absorb it, and to use this as the springboard for effective, purposeful action. This is helpful not only at work but in your personal life too.

Consider some situations in which using Questioning will enable you to be even more successful. For example, Questioning to:

- Find out information – to generate quality solutions, achieved first time, without difficulties and false starts along the way

- Provide what the client really wants – which starts by finding out from the client what they really want

- Take charge of your own development – through, for example, tapping into the skills of those around you, getting quality feedback, exploring new possibilities

- Build relationships – through understanding others' points of view, establishing contact with them and mutual Positive Regard

- Get what you want – things you want won't automatically just come your way, but asking, 'Can I?' is a polite and assertive way of stating a request rather than a demand

Good Questioning starts, of course, with good Listening. It may be no accident that we have two ears and one mouth, which, as the saying goes, should be used in that proportion!

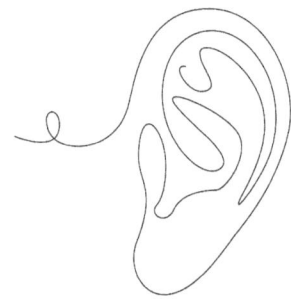

Active and Effective Listening

Active Listening does not mean keeping totally silent. You may need to check your understanding of what has been said, and whether you have actually construed its meaning.

Effective Listening is not a passive skill. If you wish to really understand what is being said, further explore the person's feelings or encourage them to say more.

There are certain attitudes and behaviours which will help you to demonstrate Active and Effective Listening.

1. Attitude

You need to be genuinely interested in what is being said and who is saying it, have Positive Regard for them and be prepared to empathise with them. Empathising does not necessarily mean agreeing with them, but understanding and respecting where they are coming from.

2. Concentration

Good listening is tiring because it requires you to make an effort to get beyond the words that are being said. You need to become attuned to the feelings and thoughts that lie behind the words. This is possible by concentrating on the listening process and not allowing yourself to be distracted, either by outside events or by your own thought processes.

It is all too easy to allow yourself to start judging what is being said, or to start preparing your next intervention or question. Whenever possible, just allow yourself to absorb the content like a sponge, storing away any points which you perhaps need to explore further at the appropriate time.

3. Non-Verbal Behaviours

Appropriate non-verbal behaviours show the speaker that you are genuinely listening. The following list briefly explains the non-verbal signals that are demonstrated by the best listeners. When used naturally, they can help generate the desired feelings of understanding, empathy and non-evaluative acceptance:

- Posture – alert and attentive without invading the speaker's personal space. Often the listener's posture will mirror the speaker's when Active Listening is taking place.

- Eye contact – the speaker needs you to be there with eye contact when they look at you, but not boring into them and not a glassy-eyed stare. Many speakers look away from you while they are

SKILL 2: SEEKS CLARITY – WHY, WHAT AND HOW?

collecting their thoughts. This is not to do with 'shiftiness' and it is important that you are 'there' when they return to you.

- Nodding and 'grunting' – to show understanding and to encourage the speaker to say more. A limited use of nodding and 'uh-huhs' is useful, although too much can give the impression of wanting to hurry the speaker along or can become irritating to them.

- Appropriate facial expressions – if you are in there with them, allow empathy to show in your face. A smile, a frown or look of concern at the right time is powerful in demonstrating you are listening.

4. Paraphrasing

Active Listening, as you know, does not mean keeping totally silent. You may need to check your understanding of what has been said, or whether you have accurately construed their meaning. Rephrase what the speaker has said in your own words, using phrases like, 'As I understand it, what you're saying is...', or 'Do you mean that... ' – avoid repeating their words parrot-fashion.

5. Reflecting underlying feelings

Truly Effective Listening goes beyond simply hearing the spoken word, in that it is perceptive to the feelings involved. Test the accuracy of your perception with phrases such as, 'I suppose that must have been awkward for you' or 'I guess that really annoyed you'. If you are right, the speaker is encouraged by your understanding and feels able to say more. If you are wrong, it can provoke further clarification along the lines of, 'I wasn't annoyed, more frustrated by what had happened' or 'Annoyed? I was absolutely steaming!'

6. Summarising

If you are listening to something detailed or complex, it may be necessary for you to ask the speaker to pause so that you can break up what you are hearing into manageable chunks. Use phrases like, 'Hang on, what we've got so far is...' or, 'OK, so the order of events was...' This ensures you have picked up and stored away, in digestible amounts, what is being said, and allows you to concentrate on the rest without embarking on major feats of memory.

7. Spotting signals

Occasionally, the speaker will drop signals into the conversation, which can be particularly useful. If you can, pick up on them and explore them more thoroughly:

- Trailing sentences – look for the 'trailing off' at the end of a sentence as it can often speak volumes. For example, 'How is the team doing?' might be answered with, 'Well, they are all working hard on their individual work...' Their tone of voice could well be giving you the clue that, while the individual work is fine, teamwork may be a problem.

- Stopping for a reaction – it is natural for the speaker to stop when they have just made a significant point. They are often looking to you for a response, which will encourage them to go on. If you leap in with your own views at that point, you may miss their signal. Instead, say something like, 'OK, that sounds important, say some more', or, 'I've got some thoughts on that which we'll come back to – I'm interested to hear more from you on that'.

- The throwaway line – listen particularly to things people say as they are about to leave. These may be things they have been trying to get around to saying but haven't found the opportunity to do so.

- Key words – listen for key words, possibly words that they emphasise, which warrant some further exploration. For example, 'I've had some difficulty in coming to terms with the new system, but they are only minor concerns, nothing to worry about.'

Active Listening does not include probing questions of a cross-examination type such as 'Why did you do that?', or 'What are you going to do about it?' These types of question cause control of the discussion to shift away from the speaker and potentially useful information may therefore be lost.

It is inevitable that you will need to ask some questions at some stage, but not at the expense of the speaker's flow. Avoid using their words like a flow of traffic, waiting for a gap so you can cross with your own questions. Go with the flow and suspend judgement until the traffic has passed.

There are various levels of listening, which you will probably have experienced at some point. For instance, you may have been in a room with others who are talking, and suddenly they look at you and say, 'What do you think?' You realise your mind was elsewhere, you were only listening at a superficial level and will have to engage at a deeper level to understand what is being said. To help someone feel they have been truly listened to, when they are sharing something of importance to them, it's best to demonstrate your Active Listening by listening at the deepest level, where you are deeply tuned into the person's attitude and values. Take a look at the model below. Bringing this to your awareness helps to ground you.

SKILL 2: SEEKS CLARITY – WHY, WHAT AND HOW?

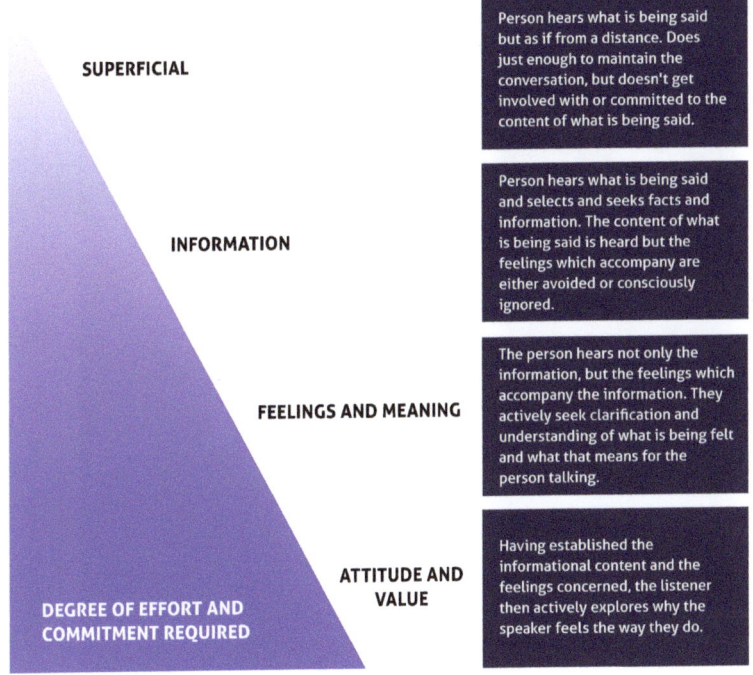

Effective Questioning

Effective Questioning requires a number of techniques which, with practice, become everyday skills exercised naturally. Like breathing, Questioning is an everyday part of life, and the correct breathing techniques help enormously when carrying out difficult exercise. And so it is with Questioning.

We shall be looking at more advanced Questioning techniques later. Let's start with the basics. Common types of questions are:

- Open Questions – these can't be answered by a simple yes or no, and are often preceded by a what, where, when, why or how, which generate much information. For example:
    - Why do you think that?
    - How would you approach the problem?
    - Where would be a good place to meet?
- Closed Questions – these limit the range of answers to yes or no. For example:
    - Do you want to take the job on?
    - Is this all right by you?
    - Shall we meet at ...?

Question	Useful	Not Useful
Leading 'You do play golf, don't you?' Invariably leads to an answer you expect	Sometimes For gaining possible acceptance of your view	Sometimes Especially if you want sound, quality information
Multiple String of questions joined together	Never	Always
Hypothetical 'What would you do if...' Posing hypothetical situations in the future	Rarely Much better to explore real situations that the person has experienced	Almost always Answers are hypothetical too
Judging 'When was the last time you did something positive to help the team as a whole?' Questions that contain judgement that the person is stupid, lazy or poorly regarded	Never	Always

There are of course other types of question commonly used, some of which have the disadvantages shown in the figure above. The building blocks of good technique, however, are open and closed questions.

Putting Open and Closed Questions to work

Open Questions encourage the other person to talk and are useful in explaining and gathering information. Sometimes the answers are not in the direction the questioner intended or are so rich in information that the questioner becomes overwhelmed or drifts off the point, particularly with talkative people. The questioner can feel out of control, and Open Questions can be quite time consuming.

Closed Questions on the other hand (for example, 'Did you agree with that?'), close the person down and can establish specific points and facts. Although seemingly time efficient, they do not explore the gaps between black and white, and also are not appropriate in emotionally charged areas.

What often happens, in practice, is that an open (divergent) question is asked. This produces a richness of information, which the questioner has difficulty in dealing with and closes that part of the conversation down with a closed (convergent) question. This is because the questioner is busy listening and at the same time trying to phrase the next question, or they feel out of control of the situation and want to bring the conversation back on track. It is also more difficult to construct Open Questions than closed ones.

However, if a questioning technique is used which starts with an open question, the response to which is followed through and explored appropriately, and the conversation then moved on or refocused to the next issue, much more can be effectively and pleasurably achieved.

Gaining Quality Information

There are three types of questions or questioning techniques that are effective in obtaining Quality Information, but they are not often used. Yet these three can make all the difference in both getting a quality result and keeping a good flow of interaction.

The first two are Probing and Refocusing, which are used for gaining clarification – Probing to draw someone out without leading them in any way, Refocusing to move them onto a different subject, with their permission. Probing and Refocusing are best used in conjunction with each other. Typically, the process is an Open question, the response to which is explored by Probing, followed by Refocusing.

The third technique is a refinement of Probing and Refocusing that takes these principles further – Critical Incident Interviewing, which we will look at in a moment.

SKILL 2: SEEKS CLARITY – WHY, WHAT AND HOW?

As we have already discussed, most people rely on Open or Closed questions, ie divergent or convergent ones, and that between these two extremes is the territory of Quality Information. The more usual sequence of questioning is an open one followed by a closed one. There are a number of reasons for this:

- Concern at being experienced as being an interrogator or too challenging.

- Having difficulty thinking up good questions, particularly open-ended ones, given the focus needed on listening to the other person. It is not easy to listen well while wondering 'What is the next question I am going to ask?'

- Concern about getting stuck on a particular line of questioning, and not being able to move the other person on without seeming unsympathetic or breaking up the flow.

- Lack of knowledge or skill about the techniques of Probing and Refocusing.

The way to overcome all this is firstly to develop a 'bank' of all-purpose 'Probes' and Refocusing questions (see the following examples). It is important that these are translated into a form which fits you. With this 'bank' you are positioned to use the technique and develop the skills, and you will feel more comfortable and confident about Probing appropriately. You will also be able to concentrate on the other person's replies, without concerns about framing the next question getting in the way.

For data collection, a good general rule is to start with an open question, followed by a couple of probes and then a refocus, so the process can start again. The number of probes used will, of course, vary according to the situation, but too many or too few both have their dangers. The biggest danger of all, though, is to not use probes at all, or badly, when trying to get Quality Information.

Here are some examples of general purpose 'Probes':

- To keep the person talking:
  - 'OK?'
  - 'Could you expand on that?'
  - 'Could you say a bit more about that?'

- To get concrete examples:
  - 'Can you give me an example?'
  - 'What did they actually do?'
  - 'Are there any more instances like that you could tell me about?'

- To find out feelings and reactions:
  - 'How do you feel about that?'

SKILL 2: SEEKS CLARITY – WHY, WHAT AND HOW?

— 'What did you think about that?'

— 'How did you cope with that?'

Examples of Refocusing questions:

- 'Can we move on to look at... now?'
- 'I'd also like to talk about... if that's OK?'
- 'OK, I understand what you are saying, but let's think about the future now.'
- 'What do you think you could do to overcome that problem?'

Now, we move onto the third technique of Critical Incident Interviewing. This type of questioning is a particularly powerful way of collecting data and can be used for a variety of purposes. It is highly structured and lends itself to those situations where it is necessary to get meaningful information in a relatively short time.

The interviewer can, by using the basic steps, encourage the interviewee to tap into real events and their experience of them, and avoid hypothetical answers coloured by what the interviewee thinks the interviewer wants to hear.

The information derived using this process is genuine and is likely to be specific and explicit, thereby providing maximum benefit.

To illustrate the process, the following is an example of someone needing to gather data from a colleague (A) on the performance of a third party (X).

1. Establish the framework	Explain that you need to elicit some information about X and that you would value A's thoughts. Check that A has had dealings with X in recent months and, if possible, find out the frequency - eg, once in the last six months or every month for the last year.
2. Create real recollections	Ask A to think back over their dealings with X. Identify, if possible, two instances that were good, had a positive outcome, produced the required end result, or went well. It is not necessary for A to tell you what these were, it is just for A to bring these to the forefront of their mind. Next ask A to think of an instance or instances in their dealings with X that were less good, less productive.
3. Establish the differences	Starting with the positive instances, ask how they differed from the less positive example(s). Allow A to continue. Then return to one difference and find out: • 'What did X actually do?' • 'What did X actually say?' Probe for specific examples of behaviour that contributed to the positive view held by A. Having explored three or four positive areas, ask A about the less positive instances. How were they different from those already discussed? Again, allow a free rein, and then return to each topic to establish specific examples.
4. Summarise	After each topic, summarise what you have noted down, then add any additional information or clarification that A gives you following your summary.

There is no need for great originality during this process. If necessary, use the same question structure repeatedly. This is not a gentle conversation over a coffee, but a concentrated, non-threatening process to obtain maximum information in the minimum amount of time.

By directing the interviewee down the paths of actual experience, and by concentrating on the areas in which you are particularly interested, you make it considerably easier for them to focus on what is real and relevant. The alternative, 'How do you think X has done this year?', leaves A floundering for something to say. When A finally does say something, it is likely to be general and bland.

The Critical Incident Interviewing technique can be used for a variety of purposes:

- Seeking feedback
- Determining expectations and defining levels of performance
- Deriving competencies
- Establishing motivation indicators (through the exploration of good and bad experiences of previous jobs)
- Selection interviews

Whenever you are going to use the process, you will need to spend a little time preparing the questions you will be asking and consider the range of experiences that you will be exploring. It is desirable to keep the Questioning as simple as possible, because this helps to speed the process and prevents the interviewee from getting side-tracked.

As with most skills, your competency and comfort will increase with practice and refinement.

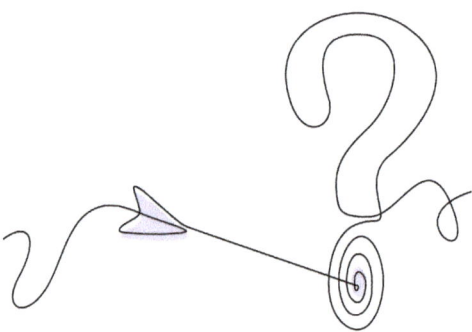

Skill 3: Negotiates for Success

> Understanding your own bias towards influencing, negotiating and conflict resolution; being skilled in a range of powerful negotiation strategies to achieve win-win outcomes for all.

In our second of the three Secrets at this part of the 6-Point Plan, we delve into a range of powerful skills and strategies to enable you to influence and negotiate well. It will also help you to manage conflict and know how to best resolve any situation you find yourself in.

Positive Negotiation and conflict management

The start to Positive Negotiation is the ability to be able to both negotiate and manage conflict well, which is where we will start with this Skill.

Negotiation and conflict are an everyday part of working life. By Negotiation we are not referring to commercial negotiation such as purchasing, although some of the same principles apply, but to those everyday occurrences where you may encounter different views, priorities and goals. This can happen with your manager, colleagues and at home. Rather than 'suffering in silence', allowing events to prove the other person wrong or cause them to 'throw their teddy out of the pram', The Pioneer uses Responsible Initiative to proactively resolve these issues, both in their own interests and those of the other people concerned.

Examples of such issues include:

- Conflicting priorities in scheduling work
- How to progress certain tasks
- What constitutes a successful project outcome
- Which pub to go to
- Whether to have Chinese or Indian food
- Where to go on holiday

Positive Negotiation is so called because the intent is to have a positive outcome, hopefully a win-win solution. This is achievable more often than not. If negotiations are less than positive, the downside is that a successful outcome may not be achieved. In this situation there is less satisfaction, maybe low self-esteem, and stress of the passive 'absorb it' kind.

Stress is also an output of conflict, if that conflict is not proactively managed. As we shall see, neither stress nor conflict can be avoided, in the workplace at

SKILL 3: NEGOTIATES FOR SUCCESS

least. What matters is how they are dealt with. Both have the upside of changing the status quo to get a better result. Non-self-directing approaches mean that one becomes a passive victim of such situations. The Pioneer's approach provides much more potential for influencing the situation productively.

It is good to know how to adapt your Negotiating Style for greater personal effectiveness. Many find their style reflects their personality style and can lead to an over-use of a less than helpful style of negotiating. Review the following Negotiating Styles and reflect on when it is best to use each one, as well as making a concerted effort to develop your use of the most positive of all Negotiating Styles – a style we call 'Co-operating'.

Negotiation styles

Competing. This represents a battling, hard-nosed style, often typical of warring parties, possibly some husband and wife arguments, with both parties striving hard to achieve their objectives, showing little co-operation towards each other. This style could be justified if, for example, unpopular courses of action such as cost-cutting have to be undertaken, or in emergencies when time does not permit other approaches.

Co-operating. This appears the most desirable style to adopt in negotiations where alongside high assertiveness and determination to achieve objectives, high levels of co-operation are displayed in seeking a solution acceptable to all parties. This Co-operating style is best illustrated in a situation where two parties who are each pursuing their own, different objectives and advocating different courses of action, talk through the issues in a constructive, co-operative fashion and develop a new course of action which permits both sets of objectives to be achieved. While generally this is the preferred style for negotiating over major issues, there may be certain situations when each of the other four styles can be justified.

Compromising. This represents a middle-of-the-road style. The person who adopts this style often enjoys both giving and taking, and the tactics of bargaining in reaching positions of compromise. It is often the case, however, that other factors may determine the use of this style. The Compromising style may be adopted if the issue under consideration does not justify the use of greater assertion associated with the Competing and Co-operative approaches. If both parties have roughly equal power and status but are pursuing opposite objectives, then the Compromising approach to negotiation may be the only realistic option.

Avoiding. The kind of person who adopts this approach is likely to feel uncomfortable when facing negotiating situations, preferring to avoid the problem of resolving differences through negotiation. In some situations, this may be the right thing to do, if it is felt that

SKILL 3: NEGOTIATES FOR SUCCESS

the dangers of confronting the differences outweigh the benefits.

Accommodating. This is very much the 'nice guy' approach in which the individual shows a high degree of co-operation towards the other party, but is often ready to yield on objectives, giving way to the other party. This approach could be justified if the issue over which the negotiations are taking place is viewed as trivial. By yielding to the other party social credits may be generated, which can be used in subsequent negotiations on more important issues.

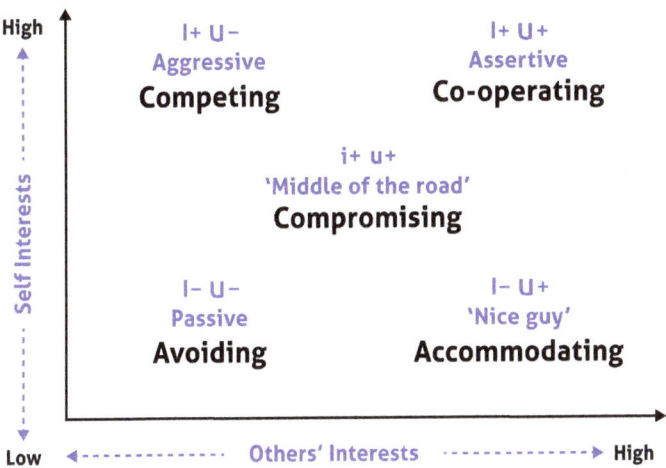

When you have reviewed the above styles, you will probably find that you will have both a preferred style and a back-up one inclining towards pursuing your own interests or allowing others' interests to take precedence if your preferred style is not working.

The ideal style, of course, is Co-operating, as this results in a win-win outcome. To achieve this requires some 'hard' skills (assertiveness), as well as some 'soft' ones (Listening), used in combination. It also requires the flexibility of problem-solving and being open to finding new creative ways to ensure the best outcome for all.

A common difficulty, in the UK particularly, is that Compromise has a cultural value as a good thing, so it is often seen as a preferred negotiation style. Both parties get something of what they want resulting in a weak win-win, and some easing of conflict. However, when compared with the large win-win and probable new or creative solutions of Co-operating, it is limited in its potential. Co-operation in this sense is akin to strategic partnership, more effort initially but with a much bigger payoff. So, in many, if not most situations, it is the preferred initial style, and if your present one is Compromising, try to shift your horizon and redirect your energy to the Co-operating primary style.

Another common cultural difficulty is that Competing has a strong value in our society, as it is aligned with winning, to the extent it becomes a personal contest, where the emotions take over, rather than being concerned with the issues. Being 'beaten' has certain consequences in negotiation for the other party, who will not see it as positive. Win-lose outcomes have a habit of being deflected into lose-lose ones. Nevertheless, there are times and situations where the particular issue

SKILL 3: NEGOTIATES FOR SUCCESS

is desperately important for you, and Co-operating is not working, when Competing, as a fallback style, is valid. However, if it's always your stance in the workplace then it's unlikely to produce consistently good, positive results.

There are times when Accommodating is sensible, for example if the issue matters to the other person but is not very important to you. It can also help in building up a fund of goodwill, which can come in useful on future occasions. However, avoid Accommodating if it results in a person being aggressive to you, this will simply encourage the other person to be more aggressive. Such aggression has to be dealt with before using the Accommodating style. The problem with Accommodating, if used too often, say as a preferred style, is that you become a 'doormat' where your own needs are never met.

Avoiding as a way of life through a preferred style is not to be recommended as nothing is resolved or achieved, and it reinforces feelings of inadequacy. This is not to say that Avoiding at times is not useful. Obvious examples are when you are not in the right mental space or do not have the time to confront the issue. The important thing is to choose to use the style, rather than just feeling you have 'wimped out'. Not everything in life has to be tackled head-on.

Choice is the operative word when using Negotiating Styles. The ideal situation is to have a Co-operating win-win orientation and the skills of Positive Negotiation to go with this, but also to be able to use other styles flexibly, depending on the situation. For example, some issues are too minor to invest time in, or you choose to:

- 'Gift' them to the other person (Accommodating)
- Not involve the family in potentially dangerous situations (Avoiding)
- Not have important principles transgressed (Competing)
- Get to a quick solution when time is of the essence (Compromising)

Your present style range is likely to be readily known to people you work with, particularly when it comes to fallback styles, which are likely to be either pursuing your own interests or learning theirs. Knowing how the other person is likely to react, and being prepared and able to deal with it, is part of Positive Negotiation.

Conflict resolution

Conflict is a daily reality for everyone. Needs and values constantly come into opposition with those of other people. Some conflicts are relatively minor, easy to handle, or capable of being overlooked. Others of greater magnitude, however, require a strategy for successful resolution if they are not to create constant tension.

Conflict resolution strategies may be classified into three categories. You'll know what stance you normally adopt when conflict arises, as you read through the categories.

Avoidance

Some people attempt to avoid conflict situations altogether or to avoid certain types of conflict. These people tend to repress emotional reactions, look the other way or leave the situation entirely. Either they cannot face up to such situations, or they do not have the skills to negotiate them effectively. On occasion, avoidance strategies do have a value - where the outcome is simply not worth bothering about, or where a lose:win will be the most probable result, but they usually do not result in a high level of satisfaction. They tend to leave doubts and fears about meeting the same type of situation in the future, and about such 'valued' traits as courage or persistence. Much depends on whether the choice made was a conscious one, or whether the remaining feeling is one of lack of resolution.

Defusion

This tactic is essentially a delaying action. Defusion strategies try to cool off the situation, at least temporarily, or to keep the issues so unclear that attempts at resolution are improbable. Resolving minor points while avoiding or delaying discussion of the major problem, postponing a confrontation until a more auspicious time and avoiding clarification of the salient issues underlying the conflict are examples of defusion. Again, as with avoidance strategies, such tactics work when delay is possible, but they typically result in feelings of dissatisfaction, anxiety about the future and concerns about oneself.

Confrontation

The third major strategy involves an actual confrontation of conflicting issues or difficulties in personal relationships. Confrontation can further be subdivided into power strategies and negotiation strategies. Power strategies include the use of physical force (a punch on the nose, war) and punishment (withholding love, recognition, money). Such tactics are often effective from the point of view of the 'successful' party in the conflict - he wins, the other person loses. Unfortunately, for the loser, the real conflict may have only just begun. Hostility and anxiety are the by-products of these win:lose power tactics.

Moving deeper into the Confrontation style of conflict resolution, it would be useful to look at a Powerful Negotiation Strategy next, which always works better than a power struggle.

Powerful Negotiation Strategy

Successful conflict resolution requires the use of a Powerful Negotiation Strategy to resolve things as follows, which can be learned and practised. This Strategy is:

1. **Diagnosis:** the ability to determine the nature of the conflict
2. **Initiation:** effectiveness in initiating resolution
3. **Listening:** the ability to hear the other's point of view
4. **Problem-solving:** using problem-solving processes to bring about a decision

1. Diagnosis

Diagnosing the nature of a conflict is the starting point in any attempt at resolution through negotiation. The most important issue to be decided is whether the conflict is an 'ideological' (*value*) conflict, or a 'real' (*tangible*) conflict – or a combination of both. Value conflicts are exceedingly difficult to negotiate, and workable solutions are only likely to come from concentrating on the tangible issues or effects of the conflict.

The reality is often that neither person needs to change their values to come to a mutually acceptable resolution of the 'real' problem, which is more about what people do (their behaviour). All too often, though, progress gets stuck in the swamp of conflicting values, without the tangible issues being allowed to surface.

So, having determined whether a conflict is real or a value conflict, and you find if it is to do with values resulting in non-tangible effects on either party, then it is best tolerated. If, however, a tangible effect exists, that element of the conflict should be resolved.

2. Initiation

The second stage in conflict resolution is effectiveness in raising the issue to initiate a resolution. It is important not to begin by attacking or demeaning the other person. The most effective way to confront the other person is for you to state the tangible effects the conflict has on you. For example, 'I have a problem – due to your stand on hiring women executives, I am unable to apply for the supervisory position that I feel I am qualified to handle'. This approach is more effective than saying, 'You male chauvinist pig – you're discriminating against me'. In other words, confrontation is not synonymous with verbal attack.

3. Listening

Once Initiation has been made, you must be demonstrably willing to hear the other person's point of view. If your position on the issue is a surprise to the other person, or is not what they were hoping to hear, defensive rebuttals, a 'hard line' approach or explanations can often result. Avoid argument-provoking replies at this stage, or defending yourself, explaining your position or making demands or threats. Instead, concentrate on Active Listening.

Reflect and paraphrase or clarify the other person's stand. When the other person's position has been interpreted to your satisfaction, then present your own point of view, being careful to avoid value statements and concentrating on tangible outcomes. Usually, when you really listen to the other person, that person is, in turn, more ready to hear another point of view. Of course, if both people are skilled in Active Listening, the chances of successful negotiation are much more likely.

4. Problem-solving

The final stage necessary for successful resolution is the use of the problem-solving process to negotiate an outcome. The steps in this process are:

- Clarifying the problem: 'What is the tangible issue?' 'Where does each party stand on the issue?'

SKILL 3: NEGOTIATES FOR SUCCESS

- Generating and evaluating a number of possible solutions: Keep problems clear of the values arena, and instead concentrate on actions and behaviour. Be creative and imaginative – this is the way most problems are unblocked.

- Concentrating on achieving a win-win outcome: Helping each person to achieve mostly what they want. This does not necessarily need to be a 'weak' win-win, because that is a compromise. Rather, depending on how well you have listened to the other person to truly understand what is important to them, and depending how creative you can be, it is often possible to get to a 'third' solution, that is better in quality than the originally proposed ones.

- Making proposals about a solution: A useful technique here, sometimes called 'third party negotiation', is to propose, for instance, 'If I do (this), will you do (that)?' This again focuses on tangible outcomes or behaviours, not values. It is possible to jointly plan the implementation of the solution and 'contract' with each other to carry it out.

Skill 4: Builds Strategic Business Acumen

> Skilfully thinking strategically, as well as tactically and operationally. You have nous and actively manage your manager; you solve problems and appreciate the culture you are working in.

This is the final Skill in The Secrets part of the 6-Point Plan. It is a skill which is rarely taught – the Skill of Building Strategic Business Acumen. Once you know what it entails, it then becomes a matter of choice. It is simply a shift in mindset, and a willingness to think more widely. Critically, it is one of the most important markers for success and will help you raise your standards of performance exponentially. This Skill helped the Pioneers in our research to shine above the rest.

What is Strategic Business Acumen?

We can describe Strategic Business Acumen as having nous. But what does nous mean? It involves seeing the work carried out not as something isolated, but part of a bigger picture, which not only gives it meaning and connection to the whole, but also allows you to spot opportunities. For example, tasks are generally one of three kinds: operational, tactical or strategic:

- **Operational:** The implementation or execution of bits of work, sometimes routine and 'proceduralised'. All our work involves some of this, and sometimes it is the main part. The timescale is short term.

- **Tactical:** Organising and planning how work is to be done and the resources it will require. It involves co-ordinating and project managing the work. The timescale is medium term.

- **Strategic:** Seeing the wider meaning and ramifications of a task and how it fits into the 'big picture'. In this way, dovetailing can be better achieved and new opportunities taken advantage of – perhaps for improved methods, outcomes, customer satisfaction or increased business.

The Pioneer may be at the early stages of their career. What marks them out is the ability to not only carry out the operational part of their work competently, and to organise it, but to do so in the context of seeing those tasks in a wider, strategic sense. They know how their work fits into the jigsaw of the whole, and in a way where difficulties and problems are anticipated and managed, and importantly where added value is created. This is nous!

It really doesn't matter what level you are at in any organisation, whether you are the cleaner or the

SKILL 4: BUILDS STRATEGIC BUSINESS ACUMEN

managing director, whatever your job title, anyone can have nous.

Here are two age-old stories to demonstrate this.

The first is from the era of Apollo 11, and President Kennedy had set the vision and promise to land a man on the Moon and return him safely by the end of the 1960s. In 1962, on a visit to NASA's command centre for a briefing, going round, the President noticed a janitor with a broom. He approached him and said, 'Hi, I'm Jack Kennedy. What are you doing?'

'Well, Mr President,' the janitor said, 'I'm helping to put a man on the Moon.'

At the time, pretty much every employee in NASA understood this vision, and how their role contributed to the whole, it was an exciting, ground-breaking time.

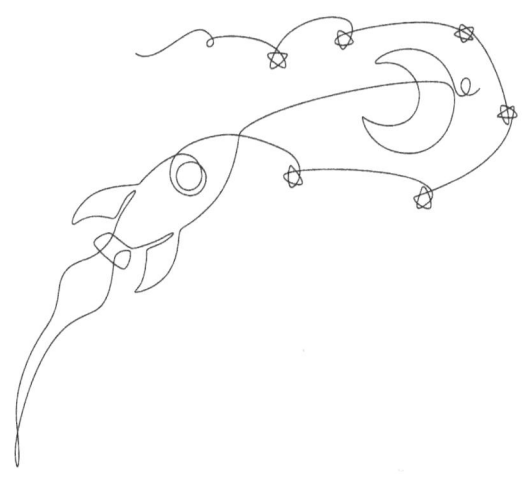

In her book, *A Dictionary of Quotations*, Louise Bush-Brown tells the story of how English architect Christopher Wren walked unrecognised to the men under his employ working on St. Paul's cathedral.

'What are you doing?' he inquired of one of the workmen, who replied, 'I am cutting stone.' He put the same question to another man, who said: 'I am earning five shillings twopence a day.' The third man he addressed answered: 'I am helping Sir Christopher Wren build a beautiful cathedral.' That man had vision. He could see beyond the cutting of the stone, beyond the earning of his daily wage, to the creation of a great cathedral.

Getting clarity on what is required, and having a clear vision to work to, is of course the essential starting point, particularly with less-routine tasks and in undertaking projects, otherwise it will be a 'stab in the dark' or at best an educated guess. Focus on the *outcome* of what is required and the definition of success by getting a clear briefing, if necessary using the Questioning techniques described earlier in this chapter.

How to manage your manager

The concept of managing your manager is not heresy – it is an unspoken reality. The relationship is a two-way street if you are a Pioneer, and it is very much part of thinking more strategically.

SKILL 4: BUILDS STRATEGIC BUSINESS ACUMEN

What are your manager's (or client's) wants and needs, fears and hopes, foibles and characteristics? If they constantly need to know how a job is progressing, whether for operational purposes or because that is the way they are, take the initiative to speak to them, to give a short progress report at sufficient intervals to keep them off your back. They will soon learn to be reassured. If something happens that they will be questioned about, let them know rather than allow them to walk into a 'booby trap'. Deliver on promises made. Above all, when there is a problem they should know about, think through some possible solutions.

Complete the following checklist to analyse your manager's behaviour and work out how to get on with them better. It should also give you some ideas about how to reward your manager when they do things which you find helpful and would like them to do more of. It would be great if you then discuss your responses with your manager.

Managing my manager checklist

What does my manager want?	
What behaviour annoys my manager?	
What behaviour makes my manager feel positive?	
What rewards would my manager like?	

Tackling problems and opportunities with Responsible Initiative

A key way of helping you demonstrate a greater use of your strategic thinking ability is to present solutions, not problems. The figure below provides a helpful flowchart to help you work through any problems you have. This also applies to any opportunities that come to light. Far better to present these to your manager or colleagues having thought through how the opportunity could add value to what you do, or how a problem could best be sorted out.

Take a look at the flowchart with a specific situation in mind – it could be a problem or an interesting proposition. Work through the chart to see what action to take. Sometimes you will have to go through the process a couple of times, which takes resilience. When it comes to the final count, you will see there are just three possible outcomes:

- You don't want to solve the problem, so adopt coping strategies, avoid moaning… move on.
- You try and solve the problem, and get stuck, but don't want to ask for help again, so change jobs… move on.
- You do manage to solve the problem, so celebrate… and move on!

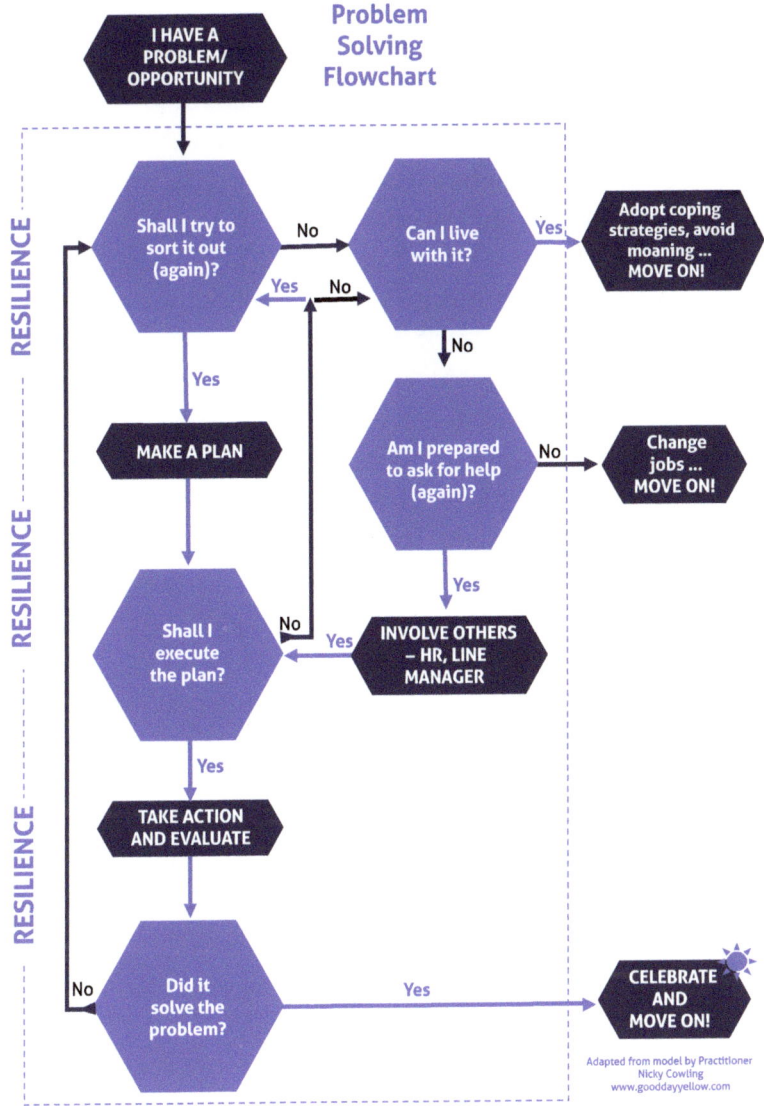

Organisation culture

Part of Building Strategic Business Acumen is about understanding the culture of your organisation. Simply put, this is the 'way things are done around here'. Each organisation is different, perhaps in subtle ways, but the differences are still important.

Culture involves not only what is done, but how it is done – the rules of engagement, so to speak. Is there, for instance, a particular style of dress, a way of presenting communications to the outside world, a particular standard adhered to, that sets it apart from other organisations? Knowing whether the culture is consistent with your values and knowing whether you need to look elsewhere for work is also important.

SKILL 4: BUILDS STRATEGIC BUSINESS ACUMEN

Chapter summary

Skill 2: Seeks Clarity – why, what and how?

The Pioneer:

- Has learned some refined skills, which enable them to obtain Quality Information quickly and well... to hear it, absorb it, and to use it as the springboard for effective, purposeful action

- Understands that Effective Listening is not a passive skill and is alert to different levels of Listening, and Listening appropriately according to the situation

- Makes good use of Effective Questioning, is skilled at using the right balance of open and closed questions, and knows how to gain Quality Information by using the more advanced techniques of Probing, Refocusing and Critical Incident Interviewing; they suspend judgement, preferring to find out the actual facts

Skill 3: Negotiates for Success

The Pioneer:

- Understands that Negotiation and conflict are part of everyday life, and takes action to build their skill in this area

- Makes practical use of Positive Negotiation to consistently create win-win outcomes, minimising the effects of stress; they are skilled at using a range of styles and they focus, where possible, on using the most effective of all styles – the Co-operating style
- Knows there is a Powerful Negotiation Strategy to bring about conflict resolution through confronting issues well and dealing with them.

Skill 4: Builds Strategic Business Acumen

The Pioneer:

- Has nous… and takes time to reflect on the operational, tactical and strategic parts of their role; they understand how their part fits into the wider picture
- Knows how to manage their manager well, so that they add value and develop a great working relationship
- Appreciates the need to effectively solve problems and knows the culture of the organisation and their role in supporting this culture

THE GEAR CHANGE: PERFORMING AT A HIGHER LEVEL

Skill 5: Controls Own Workload
Using Responsible Initiative to manage your work
Recognising problematic traits
Managing stress
Common timewasters

Skill 6: Manages Own Learning
Investing in your own business
Learning and change
Dealing with mistakes productively
Seeking and receiving feedback well
Chapter summary

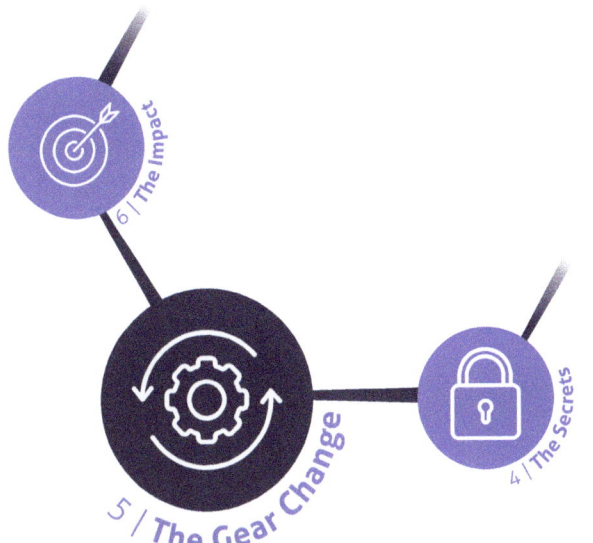

'The size of your success is measured by the strength of your desire, the size of your dream, and how you handled disappointment along the way.'
— Robert Kiyosaki

Skill 5: Controls Own Workload

> Being in control of your workload profile by recognising and managing known behavioural traits which can trip you up; you manage stress well and are acutely aware of your own Achilles Heel, taking action to counter this.

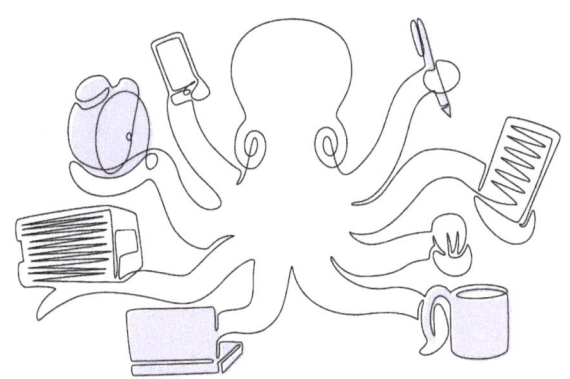

Here we are at The Gear Change, the fifth point on our 6-Point Plan. We have learned four of The Pioneer Skills, and now with Skills five and six we start Performing.

If you have been working on the earlier Skills, it means you now have the capacity to take control of any day-to-day things that have previously been getting in your way. So, if you are ready to perform and shine, let's go!

Using Responsible Initiative to manage your work

Imagine for a moment that you are leading a work team. Perhaps one member of your team is in Dependency, treating you as though you were their mum or dad. They expect you to solve all their problems – work, relationships, their career, whatever. It may be flattering, despite being wearisome, and may appeal to some part of you; you may feel a sense of protectiveness towards them. But when there is a need to streamline the department, the cold reality is they will be an early candidate for removal rather than progression.

Another team member might take lots of initiative, but too often they are the wrong ones and cause immense difficulties for you and others. This team member may have many admirable qualities – energy, enthusiasm, drive – but it is like managing a loose cannon or a rebellious teenager. You can't yet trust them to do the right things.

SKILL 5: CONTROLS OWN WORKLOAD

The majority of your team are good workers – conscientious, reasonable and courteous with other people. However, when compared with the perhaps one or two higher performers you have, there is a crucial difference.

The difference is that the higher performers operate with Responsible Initiative and are self-directing in managing their work. They anticipate problems and find solutions to them, knowing when to involve or consult you. They work proactively and productively with other people. They are clear about what needs to be achieved and manage their own workload and deadlines. They add value rather than just completing a task. They are of course technically accomplished, but they are far more than that, as they are able to translate this into value-added outcomes.

Recognising problematic traits

First, it is good to recognise some known problem behaviours which might be quite 'deep seated'. They relate to a mindset of Dependency and Counter Dependency, rather than self-directing attitudes. Even The Pioneer needs to pay attention to ensure they are not caught by these more problematic traits, especially when resilience is low. Reflect on them and see which one might catch you out. These problem behaviours are:

Blaming	When every problem is blamed on someone else - the organisation, boss, co-workers, the system or whatever - with no responsibility accepted for one's own capability.
Hero	Taking on everything, volunteering to come early and work late, undertaking weekend assignments, acting like superman/woman and getting worn down. The payoff is being able to cash in on feelings of being over-busy and put upon.
Because	Surely you can't expect much from me when I have such a handicap - ie wrong gender, wrong size, wrong race, wrong background, wrong state of health, etc.
I'm trying!	Don't blame me if things turn out wrong. After all, see how hard I tried (the underlying agenda is to 'try' but not achieve).

When problem traits like this are brought out into the open, they can be spotted and dealt with. It gives us a choice, to either sink into that trait or take action to move on. You know what The Pioneer would do!

Managing stress

Staying in control of your own workload is a key part of being a Pioneer. Clearly, rushing round in a panic, failing to deliver what has been promised, creating more problems rather than finding solutions, is hardly a recipe for success, and leads to unnecessary stress. It is a world away from the purposeful and effective performance of those who achieve reliably and well. Unless one is addicted to self-induced stress, being out of control is not a good place to be, with consequences

SKILL 5: CONTROLS OWN WORKLOAD

for how you are regarded, your capability for possible promotion, let alone the energy you have left for your personal life.

There is all the difference in the world between feeling stretched and challenged, where you are working in the 'flow', effectively and efficiently, and when you feel hurried, always stretching to catch up on out-of-control events. This introduces the notion of stress.

Stress is both a good thing and a bad thing – too little and we Rust Out, too much and we Burn Out.

The positive side of stress is stimulus, such as responding to challenges, with the buzz that can result. Another perspective is that the only time we won't ever encounter some stress is when we are dead!

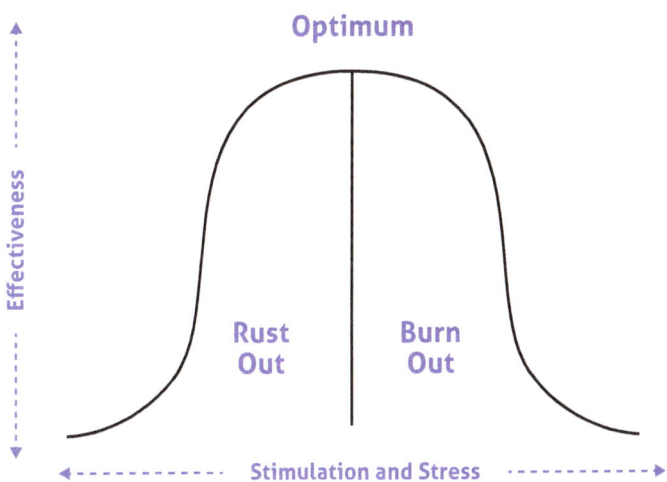

The Pioneer's approach to stress is through managing their own stress environment, which includes knowing what kind of stress is productive for you and what is not, and what works for you in terms of the way you handle it.

In terms of being able to handle stress, you have to know what works for you. For some it might be meditation, for others, physical activity and exercise; for yet others seeking help from colleagues or friends. It is important to know what to do, to prevent Burn Out when you are feeling overwhelmed.

Being self-directing in this way also means that you will take a deliberate conscious view of what you want if you encounter one of the phenomena of today's 'macho stress culture'. Do you play or don't you play? Either decision will have consequences which you will need to face up to and resolve.

It is not intended here to deal with stress in a more complete way, largely because there are many other texts available which will cover it, but it is clearly a factor which has to be taken into account in Controlling Your Own Workload. This is also more than just time management. Time management is to do with how efficiently you spend your time, and there are many structured ways of managing this, which work in various ways for different people.

SKILL 5: CONTROLS OWN WORKLOAD

Controls Own Workload is a much wider view of how you manage your job, not just your time. It involves taking responsibility for managing yourself and negotiating timescales. It also requires us to be honest with ourselves about the kind of person we are (see Chapter 1: Part 1, The Mirror), recognising where our problems lie and using Responsible Initiative to do something about them. We may, for example, be a person who likes to button things down quickly – fine, but there may be useful information to come. Or we may prefer to keep everything fluid until the deadline approaches – also fine, but this tends to result in last minute panic.

Knowing how we tend to respond allows us to use our strengths and manage our weaknesses. Use the list below to identify what is most likely to be holding you back.

Common timewasters

Procrastination	Putting things off, particularly unpleasant tasks, or putting off making decisions even though they have been considered plenty of times.
Disorganisation	Not knowing where to find things, not being clear where to start and what to do, creating own chaos.
Not prioritising	Doing what comes to hand, or is pleasant and easy to do, rather than what is important or urgent.
Estimating time poorly	Not having an accurate time estimation of how long a task will take, including not allowing for interruptions, problems, etc.
Too willing to help others out	Being over-willing to help others at the expense of own work commitments.
Interruptions	Not managing to get into the 'flow' of work because of interruptions, necessary or not.
Not anticipating problems	Being taken by surprise by problems instead of anticipating them in advance.
Being impulsive	Acting when the whim takes you rather than on a more methodical basis.
Unable to say 'No'	Doing everything that comes your way, not being able to use positive negotiation to decide priorities, timescales, etc.
Losing track	Losing sense of what must be done and by when in the flurry of activities.

Skill 6: Manages Own Learning

> Investing in your own business as a way of life, knowing that learning is a cycle of change. You treat mistakes as a learning opportunity and understand the importance of seeking and receiving feedback, while knowing the parameters for success.

As you feel the shift in gear required for this step of the Three Critical Steps (see Chapter 2), you will appreciate that you are the captain of your ship. It is up to you how far and fast you want to develop. No one cares as much about your learning and growth as you do.

Investing in your own business

There is an old adage: 'Give a man a fish, and you feed him for a day. Teach a man to fish and you feed him for a lifetime.'

It is the same with learning and development. The Pioneer has learned, so to speak, to fish for themselves, while Dependent people are more likely to expect the organisation to take charge of their training and development.

The Pioneer sees the need to invest in their own business and success by taking an active approach to their own learning and continuous development. This is not just through taught courses, they use their everyday work environment to actively learn. Also, it is more than just through experience on the job, it is the way they make best use of that experience which really matters. They also do not rely just on enhancing their technical expertise, but on the way it is carried into effect. They use change as a learning opportunity.

In particular, they:

- Understand how to actively learn as a process
- Seek and use feedback well, and understand why this is important

- Deal with mistakes productively
- Establish for themselves what is required for success

Learning and change

Change is another word for learning. Those who are already learning, continuously, are the people who can ride the waves of change. Change does not have to be forced on us by crisis or calamity, rather it is part of continuous learning. What it does require, however, is for each one of us to take charge of our own learning. It requires a Growth Mindset to achieve what you desire, where you are open to possibilities, to different ways of thinking and being.

We all assume that we know how we learn. Often the assumption is based on being taught. However, learning is:

- A cycle of different activities
- A double loop process, which involves both solving the particular problem and developing the habit of learning
- Best carried out in 'real life'
- A process of discovery, where we must each be our own discoverer

All this requires us, as individuals, to take Responsible Initiative for managing our own learning and development, for receiving and dealing with feedback well and proactively, for harnessing the realities of everyday work experience to learn and grow. Learning is a cycle in that it is like a wheel that is kept in motion by a series of jolts – the faster the wheel or cycle moves, the faster we learn. In this cycle there are four stages, each one of them important for real learning.

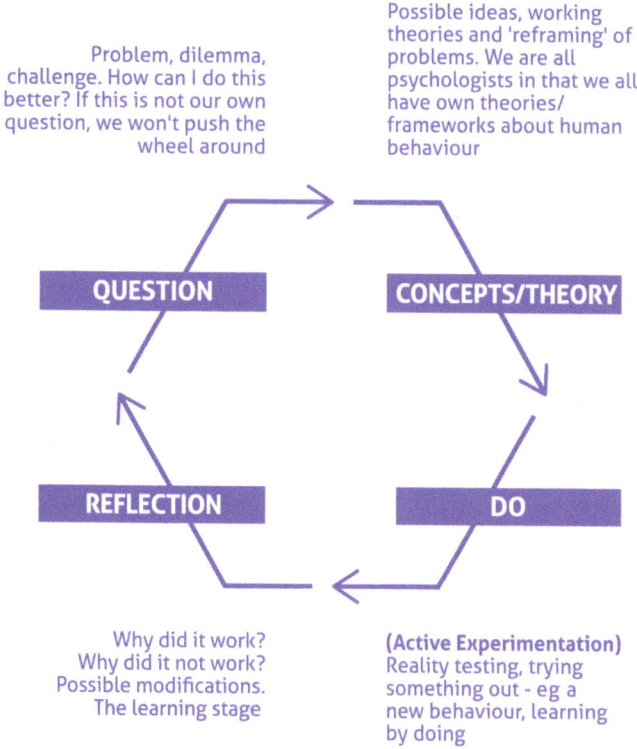

When you look at the Learning Cycle it seems obvious... it is. Most people, however, are more comfortable

SKILL 6: MANAGES OWN LEARNING

with, and thus tend to use more, particular stages of the cycle. Really effective learners have well developed skills for each stage of the process or know themselves sufficiently well to be aware of what they tend to neglect, and thus compensate for it. For example, Reflection is an area that often gets missed. Equally, some people can get stuck in one or other stage of the cycle or take short cuts across it. For instance, jumping from the Question straight into action, then straight back to the next Question. Take a look and see what you think.

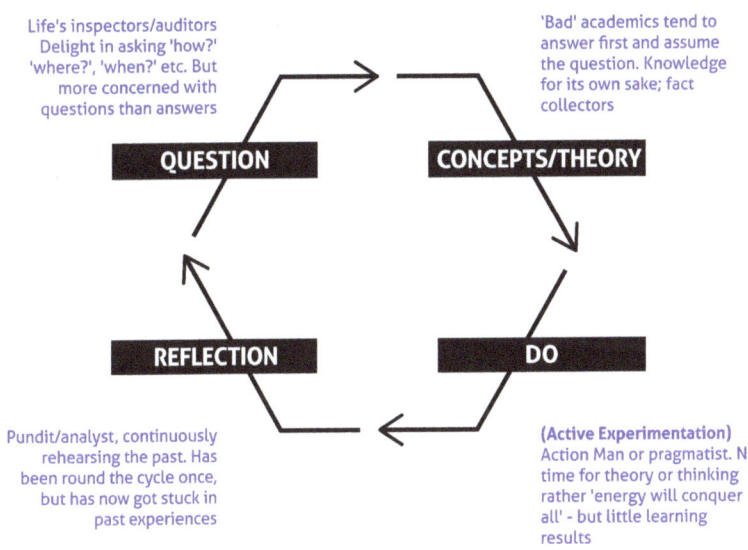

The great Irish author, philosopher and specialist in organisational behaviour and management, Charles Handy, suggests there are some necessary conditions for comfortable change and effective continuous learning:

Those who learn best, and change most comfortably:

- Take responsibility for themselves and their future
- Have a clear view of what they want that future to be
- Want to make sure they can get it, and believe they can
- Have an ability to see things/problems/situations in other ways – to 'reframe' them
- Deal with mistakes and failures without being downhearted or dismayed

They also avoid the things that can often block our way:

- The 'they' syndrome
- Fatality or humility
- The theft or leaking of their purpose
- A missing forgiveness

Dealing with mistakes productively

Many of us have been taught from an early age that mistakes are bad. Of course, those to do with being slipshod, careless or irresponsible are. But unless we make mistakes we won't learn. If we are paralysed by the fear of making mistakes, we won't try anything new. We become trapped in the comfort and security of the well tried and known and are ill-equipped to deal with change.

Another way of looking at mistakes is to see them as Positive Mistakes from which we can learn, and also that they are an inevitable part of exploration. Some companies become uneasy when their senior managers don't make any mistakes as this could be because they are not taking any risks or are unwilling to try out new initiatives.

What really matters is how mistakes are dealt with, and whether they are learned from or just repeated. The Pioneer is prepared to make 'genuine' mistakes, not deliberately, but responsibly, as part of their learning, and when they do occur see them as Positive Mistakes from which they can learn and develop. This means taking personal responsibility for them and not blaming others, over-reacting or allowing their self-esteem to be damaged, but importantly mining them for learning. It also involves seeking and receiving feedback well.

Seeking and receiving feedback well

In developing oneself and relationships with those around us, it is important for us to both give and receive feedback. This must be done with an overall mindset of Positive Regard and Genuineness with the aim of enhancing the relationship and enabling yourself and others to grow. This is The Pioneer approach, leading to true Interdependence.

There is an extremely helpful model to help us understand the importance of giving and receiving feedback. It was devised by American psychologists Jo Lufts and Harry Ingham in the 1950s while researching team working. It is aptly named the Johari Window, which we will look at next.

	Known to self	Unknown to self
Known to others	Public	Blind
Unknown to others	Private	Unknown

The model is based on the premise that an individual will know themselves, to a greater or lesser extent, and that those around them – people with whom they work, their family and friends – will also know them by what and how they say and do things.

Public Pane: This concerns that area of oneself about which there are no secrets. I might know, for example, that I am a poor planner and get irritated by what I see as unnecessary detail when deciding on a course of action. Those around me will also know this because I might tell them, or they might observe it simply from my reactions in those situations.

Private Pane: This contains those bits of self-knowledge which I choose not to broadcast or reveal. Perhaps I feel nervous when making presentations, or alternatively find confronting discipline issues difficult. Some prefer to keep their thoughts and feelings private and don't share much information about themselves.

Blind Pane: This pane is particularly significant. It contains those behaviours which others see and experience when dealing with me, but about which I am ignorant or blind. For example, I might be totally unaware of how aggressive I appear when debating a work issue, or how my habit of looking at my watch during an appraisal interview gives the impression of impatience or indifference.

Unknown Pane: The final part of the window represents the Unknown. That is, the behaviours or reactions I might have in a situation yet to be experienced.

We all have ideas about how we would handle the masked raider, but until that situation arises, no one will know, least of all me!

The people who can best manage themselves and their environment, be it at work or socially, are those who have consciously enlarged the first pane of their window. This means that the Public, open side of themselves – what they know about themselves, their strengths and weaknesses, and also what those around them know and accept – is increased and there is more about you on display.

	Known to self	Unknown to self
Known to others	Public → Ask (feedback) ↓ Tell (disclosure)	Blind
Unknown to others	Private	Unknown

SKILL 6: MANAGES OWN LEARNING

This widening of the Public Pane of the Johari Window is achieved through two clear behaviours – Disclosure and Feedback.

The Private Pane can be reduced by the simple practice of being open with others. If I am unsure of my position in a particular meeting, I can say so. Or, if I am finding a colleague's approach frustrating at a particular time, I can say so. This openness is seen as being genuine with others; they are able to see exactly what is going on and can respond accordingly.

There are some things in my Private Pane that I hold dear, and don't ever want to share, and that's absolutely fine. However, sometimes I might be viewed as cagey and unwilling to share anything personal, which is often the case for more quiet, Introverted types, or Extraverts who are too fast-paced and task-focused. So, if I can also share a little more about me, my interests and hobbies for instance, what I'm thinking and feeling, it will help to develop a greater rapport with others.

Perhaps the most valuable movement that can be made is the 'drawing back of the curtains' on the Blind Pane. This is done through seeking feedback from those around you and, crucially, the skilled reception of that feedback from the potentially unskilled giver. This means, when asking for feedback, being prepared for anything, and working from the premise that all feedback, whether good or bad, helps us to develop – it is a gift. And the only response to feedback, like receiving a gift, is 'thank you'. We will talk more about this in a moment.

Getting a clearer view of how others see us, and how our behaviour impacts on them, and then choosing how to use that information for our own development, is a powerful skill indeed. It is often the case that we are unable to hear what people are really saying to us, but it is only when we do that, that we can test out the reality of who we are and are able to grow.

With regard to the Unknown Pane, we are more rich and complex than we or others know. From time to time something will happen – maybe it is felt, heard, seen, read about or dreamed – and something from our unconscious is revealed to us. Then we know what we have never known before, as if someone has just turned on a light, enabling us to see, and this knowledge in turn enables us to grow.

> 'What lies behind you and what lies
> in front of you, pales into comparison
> to what lies inside of you.'
> — Ralph Waldo Emerson

Unfortunately, feedback or criticism is often unskilfully given, and our natural defence mechanisms swing into action, rather than seeing the feedback as a gift. This can cause us to 'shoot the messenger' instead of really hearing the message.

This is likely to be because it is ingrained in most of us, from an early age, that mistakes are bad. We have to wriggle out from under the mistake and maintain our innocence, using a range of well-worn approaches – eg 'It came off in my hand, Mum!'

As a result, we make it exceptionally difficult and frustrating for the giver, who has had to steel themselves for the task in the first place, and who leaves the interview with all their beliefs confirmed, 'There's no point in talking to him – he's so dammed prickly!'

However, it is not just people's perceptions of us that are damaged by our poor reception of feedback. We are cutting ourselves off from priceless data that we can use to really manage personal growth. There is also the danger that mistakes which we have made are not explored and learned from, and remain as 'tiger traps' for us to fall into, time and time again.

So, the first shift required is one of attitude: 'Mistakes help me become more competent, so, help me to see where I've made them'.

Below are some techniques that should ease the process of receiving feedback however it is delivered, and will also ensure that you derive the maximum benefit from the process:

- Appreciate the giver: if you recognise the difficulty the giver may be experiencing in delivering the message and appreciate their intent is to help, you will not only find it easier to suppress your 'defence mechanisms' but it will also encourage the giver to give more. Make a point of thanking them for their feedback.

- Reflecting back: make sure you are really picking up the message by reflecting back what you have heard – 'I see what you mean, my lack of preparation must have been obvious to the client.'

- Probing for examples: if you are serious about using the feedback to make changes, you need as much clarity as you can get. Probe the giver until you are sure you know what is meant – 'I'm not sure I understand – can you give me an example of when I appeared unprepared?'

- Taking action: show the giver that it has been worthwhile talking to you by telling them what you are going to do as a result of the feedback.

- Ask for further feedback: demonstrate that you value what they have said by asking them for further feedback in the future on how you are performing in the area under discussion, or other related areas.

In some situations, you may feel that you are not getting enough feedback to help you learn and develop. If this is the case, take The Pioneer approach of asking for it.

Feedback often involves both positive as well as negative feedback. Sometimes, managers are relatively unskilled at giving positive feedback and use generalised phrases such as 'I liked that', 'That was good', 'You performed well', etc. Although this may give you a warm glow and reassure you that you are going in the right direction, it is not as helpful as it might be. It is more valuable to your learning to know what aspects were liked and why, so that you can repeat them, in which case you need to probe more to understand what specifically is being valued.

Chapter summary

Skill 5: Controls Own Workload

The Pioneer:

- Uses Responsible Initiative in managing their workload – they:

  — Anticipate problems and find solutions

  — Work proactively and productively with other people

  — Are clear about what needs to be achieved and manage their own deadlines

  — Add value, rather than just completing a task

- Understands how to manage their manager, knowing their wants, fears, foibles and characteristics – they know it is a 'two-way street'
- Is good at managing their own stress levels and knows what to do to prevent Burn Out. They are acutely aware of the common timewasters which can catch them out, and take action to mitigate the risks associated with their Achilles Heel.

Skill 6: Manages Own Learning

The Pioneer:

- Sees the need to invest in their own business and success by:
  - Taking an active approach to their own learning and continuous development
  - Developing The Skills needed at each stage of the learning cycle, knowing how easy it is to get stuck along the way
  - Taking responsibility for themselves and their future; they have a clear view of what they want that future to be and believe they can achieve it
- Deals with mistakes productively, seeing them as an inevitable part of learning. They take personal responsibility for them, not blaming others, over-reacting or allowing their self-esteem to be

SKILL 6: MANAGES OWN LEARNING

damaged – they glean all the learning they can from them.

- Understands the importance of seeking and receiving feedback, even when feedback is unskilfully given – they appreciate the giver, reflect back, ask for examples and take action.

6

THE IMPACT

Skill 7: Takes Charge of Own Career
Me PLC
Avoiding the Swamp
Knowing your own motivations
Managing your own business
Writing your own business plan
The Review: Putting it all together
Step One: Preparing
Step Two: Positioning
Step Three: Performing
The Pioneer Wheel
Chapter summary

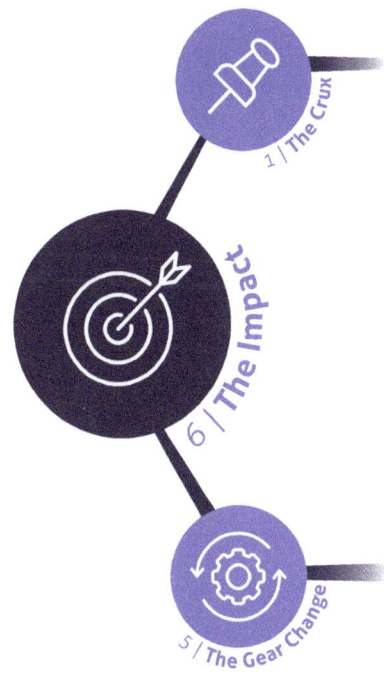

'All you need is the plan, the road map, and the courage to press on to your destination.'
— Earl Nightingale

Skill 7: Takes Charge of Own Career

> Creatively self-reliant, you know your own motivations and manage your own business well by writing your career plan, like a business plan – Me PLC. You use powerful networking skills and constantly adapt to change.

We now reach point six on The Pioneer 6-Point Plan, where we have a chance to test things out and review things. Takes Charge of Own Career is the final Skill in the Performing stage of the Three Critical Steps. This chapter will help you test things out and equip you with the tools needed to move you to action.

You may have come across the old saying, 'It's time to walk the walk'. Rather than letting the grass grow under your feet, and feeling like life is passing you by, you are now taking The Pioneer approach and consciously, purposefully charting your course to greater success and balance.

Me PLC

We are nearing the end of the book, and you know now that no one is as interested in your career as you are. Not your manager (although they may be supportive), not the organisation, no one! We are back to the point of you managing your own business, your career, in a self-directing way. Otherwise, you won't achieve what you want. This is of course supposing you know what you want. Your career is part of your life overall, so your career needs to be seen in this context. What we are talking about is both career and life planning; they are part and parcel of each other. The Pioneer approach makes a crucial difference in life overall and not just in the workplace.

Firstly, it is useful to review what is your own business (your career) and in what business context your business is now being managed. If you calculate what you expect to earn, including any fringe benefits, over your thirty to forty years of work, it is likely that you will find yourself as the managing director of a million or multi-million pound business. If your success criteria include financial ones, there are obvious implications here. But the once-in-a-lifetime opportunity to fulfil your goals, dreams and aspirations won't happen by itself.

A salutary way of thinking about this is to reflect on what your obituary will say about you, in just six words! Why don't you have a go in your notepad?

Careers are being managed in a different business context from the past, when career planning was managed by the organisation and career paths were visible and often promised. It is likely the job you will have in five years' time doesn't currently exist. In short, the context has changed where instead of taking a farming

SKILL 7: TAKES CHARGE OF OWN CAREER

approach (planting seeds in a patch of ground, nurturing them over time) a more appropriate approach today is a hunter-gatherer one, which involves looking for, and finding, the opportunities. This requires advanced preparation and having The Skills to make the best use of the opportunities through The Pioneer approach.

At the most basic level, most people's financial security comes from their ability to earn money. The first rule of warfare is said to be to protect your home base – in our terms to secure our capacity to earn a good living. This requires keeping our skills current and in tune with modern and evolving requirements. These are not just based on technical expertise but on the emotional competencies to deliver them well. Above all, it means being flexible, in coping well with new ways of working and change. It used to be said, for example, that to be a 'Jack of all trades was to be a master of none'; the requirements now are more in the direction of being a 'Jack of all trades and a master of some'.

To summarise then, at its lowest level security comes not from being employed, but from being employable, and it is in this arena that the concepts of taking responsibility for your own learning and career join forces. But this is to see it at its lowest level, albeit a fundamentally important one. If our horizon is raised above this, there is much more to play for in terms of our success, satisfaction and achievement. Is what we are experiencing at present 'as good as it gets', or could it be made to get better?

Avoiding the Swamp

The first place to start, of course, is to gain greater clarity on what you want, that is, what your own definition of success is. As the saying goes, 'If you don't know where you are going, any road will take you there'. This applies not just to your career, but your life overall – the two are intertwined.

A good number of us are caught up in the Swamp, having some vague wishes of what we want to be doing some time away out into the future. It is all very general and a long way off. For example, we may want to retire early but are making no financial provision for this. Somehow, we think it may happen by luck or by winning the lottery. Or we think that we may want to become a senior manager but feel it will be OK to learn the skills required once we have been offered the post. We are reluctant to think through specifically what we want to do, now, as the first step towards our future aims or dreams.

It's a little like the age-old myth about the boiled frog, which may or may not be true, but it serves to make a point – and please don't try this at home! It is thought that if you pop a live frog into a pot of boiling water, it has sensors in its skin which cause it to immediately jump out again to safety. However, if you pop a frog into a cold pot of water and gently boil it, it doesn't realise what's happening and loses the ability to respond quickly enough to prevent disaster.

SKILL 7: TAKES CHARGE OF OWN CAREER

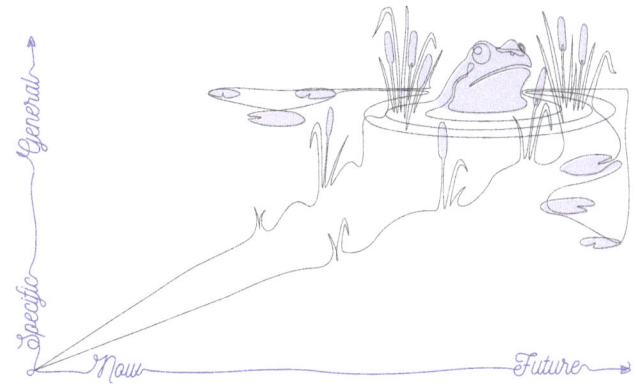

So, for people who are in the Swamp, little is likely to happen, except by chance. Luck rarely meets opportunity because there has been no preparation. The successful, achieving people know where they want to be going, and start taking specific steps now to commence their journey. They also know that they have to be flexible and adaptable, because circumstances and wants may change around them in the future, but unless they get mobilised to march in the direction they want to go, nothing will happen anyway. They successfully combine purpose and focus with adaptability, keeping their eyes open to the other opportunities and choices they discover en route.

All this focuses on 'success' and what it implies and means for you in both career and life terms. Remember, no one is as interested in your career as you are. There is an exception to this, and that is when you are living for other people's expectations – perhaps your parents, perhaps others? Getting clarity on your definition of success is the first important step in achieving that success.

For example, to start this process, which of the following do you see as the foundation for your success?

Advancement	Where you have greater responsibility, influence, status, etc, and correspondingly greater rewards. In many ways, this is the traditional definition of success.
Context and meaning	Working within an organisation that is compatible with your values and attributes, and provides a purpose and goals with which you can strongly identify.
Personal goals	Lifestyle and having a good balance between home and work. Contributing in wider society outside work.

Success could be based on all three, but in different proportions and with varying emphasis, for they are not mutually exclusive.

Knowing your own motivations

A useful tool for identifying the kind of environment that you will find most appealing, *at present*, is the Motivation Inventory (designed by Dr Derek Biddle), which we will look at next. 'At present' is stressed, because needs do change over time.

The Motivation Inventory Quick Analysis will enable you to compare what you are getting from your present job with your defined needs in the areas of People, Achievement and Enjoyment. It may be that not all your needs are being met; if this is the case, then avoid moving automatically to 'the grass is greener' syndrome and take a balanced view. Or you may be getting much of what you want, and the way ahead may be to find the missing part by taking a self-directing approach and achieving it either inside or outside work.

Do go ahead and have a look at the three Motivation Inventory categories under People, Achievement and Enjoyment. Pick out the top three motivators or statements which really matter to you – and put them in order, allocating ten points to the number one motivator of overriding importance, eight points for your second one, and six points for the third one.

Motivation Inventory Quick Analysis

PEOPLE	ACHIEVEMENT	ENJOYMENT
INFLUENCE Persuading, communicating, developing, convincing people towards a course of action	**TASK FOCUS** Having a liking for detail and analysis, using skills and knowledge, enjoying specific tasks and intellectual challenge, focusing on the job in hand	**SUITABILITY** Comfort in knowing capability to do job based on previous experience, perceived match of knowledge and skills
NURTURE Helping people achieve their goals, listening to them, providing close support as well as time and attention	**GOAL ORIENTATION** Working to targets, a future perspective to achieve tangible results, output rather than input focused, problem solving, satisfying customers and providing good service, achieving business results	**STRUCTURE** Operating to guidelines and systems, organising and planning, meeting standards, creating order, procedures and systems

PEOPLE	ACHIEVEMENT	ENJOYMENT
GREGARIOUSNESS Meeting and working with a wide range of people, including the public	**POWER & AUTHORITY** Having control over others, being able to direct them and control work and events, making big decisions, being regarded as the source of authority	**SECURITY** Job security, knowing what is going on, a liking for certainty
SOLITUDE Having space to get on with things without contact or distraction from other people	**RESPONSIBILITY** Leading others, taking and accepting responsibility for decisions, making a difference, doing what is necessary to ensure company success, representing others	**TANGIBLE REWARD** Money, status, glamour, perks
AFFILIATION Having close relationships, being part of a team, working interdependently with others and being liked and respected by them	**INITIATIVE & INDEPENDENCE** Using own initiative, dislike of bureaucracy and red tape, operating independently, deciding own course of action	**VARIETY & FUN** Enjoyment and fun, difference, travel, location, not repetitive or boring
DEDICATION Helping the company's wider society and the community, doing something worthwhile, making the world a better place	**CREATIVITY** Generating ideas, producing something new, finding new ways	**RECOGNITION** Being well regarded and appreciated, feeling good about self and work, self-development
RELATING Responding to different individual needs, dealing with difficult interpersonal situations, trusting and being trusted, resolving conflict	**CHALLENGE** Being stretched, liking energy and hard work and competitive situations, responding to pressure and deadlines being active and challenged	**COMFORT** Working moderate hours, not dealing with unpleasant or difficult situations, keeping clear of anxiety and stress, avoiding failure

SKILL 7: TAKES CHARGE OF OWN CAREER

Once you have done this, review the points below:

- Are your top three motivators in the same overall category – ie under People, Achievement or Enjoyment? If they are, this category and those particular motivators really matter to you and are currently driving you. It's important that those needs are met, otherwise you are likely to get 'itchy feet' and want to move on.

- Maybe your top three motivators are spread across the categories, or two in one category and one in a different one. If they are, then you have a range of motivators which are important, and it may be easier to get some if not all these needs met, or you may have some work to do to make things better.

- Do your primary motivators fit with your current role? If they don't, do you need to have a conversation with your leader, or yourself, to sort things out?

It may be interesting for you to note that the:

- People category is all about *others*
- Achievement category is all about the *task*
- Enjoyment category is all about *you*

Depending on your definition of success, what your goals are, what you are trying to achieve, this

Motivation Inventory will hopefully give you a chance to reflect on what is really important to you, and the action you need to take now. You might be asking yourself if the motivators are serving you well right now, or do you need to do some work on yourself. Or maybe the motivators are spot on and absolutely what drives you, and you need to celebrate you are in the right environment – or take action to change it if things are not right yet.

Managing your own business

It has been highlighted that you are running your own business, but few of us give thought or attention to preparing a business plan for our own business, although it is one of the first disciplines of running an actual business. This would be an excellent exercise for you to do and there is a plan at the end of this chapter, so you can make a start.

The world of work is now a fluid one. The idea of earlier generations, when people would have a job for life, is long gone. Loyalty just isn't enough. Job security and career management are what you make of it from your own resources, by taking The Pioneer approach to it, or not. The other side of the coin is that the spectrum of opportunity is in many ways so much larger than it was, that is for those people who have equipped themselves to make best use of it, like this:

1. **Have the mindset of managing your own business.** Keep in mind that you are the managing director of your own business – you – even when you are an employee of an organisation. This will help you to stay proactive and self-directing in managing your own career.

2. **Invest in your own business.** You wouldn't invest in a business that doesn't invest in itself, would you? So, invest in yourself by developing and enhancing your own skills, abilities and capacity to learn.

3. **Maintain visibility.** Ensure that your good work and successes are noticed. Take opportunities to demonstrate that you can make a difference and add value.

4. **Network actively.** Build your network of contacts, both within and outside your current organisation. Many career opportunities are generated this way and it is also a useful 'insurance' policy.

5. **Scan the market.** Keep abreast of what is happening in the career market (internally and externally) and developments within it. Remember though to realistically appraise what you already have.

6. **Keep 'interviewee' skills current.** The 'moment of truth' in many career opportunities is the selection interview process. It is perhaps more difficult and nerve-wracking to do oneself justice

if the process hasn't been experienced for some time. Some people even go as far as to make sure they experience a selection interview at least yearly to make sure their skills are still current and effective.

7. **Manage relationships well.** Remember, as a Pioneer, you are managing your manager as well as the other way round, and the way you deal with co-workers will be key to your success. It has been stressed that Emotional Intelligence is now regarded as supremely important in organisational life. Relying on technical ability just isn't enough.

8. **Prioritise and balance your needs.** It is a reality that it is rare indeed for anyone to have everything they want, all at the same time. The Pioneer realises this and manages their situation, prioritising and maximising certain wants while balancing others. When needs change, perhaps gradually, perhaps suddenly through a life-changing event, they are able to re-evaluate and reach a new harmony about what is most important to them now.

9. **Manage change to your advantage.** It is said that, like death and taxes, change is inevitable. And so it is. We may be able to deny it in our private lives, possibly to our detriment, but to put at risk the assets of our own business by doing so is certainly not smart. Necessary change in skills, working practices, technology, and the like are inevitable.

SKILL 7: TAKES CHARGE OF OWN CAREER

The choice is whether we can respond flexibly and work with it, rather than letting it disable us. The key to this is to seek and identify the opportunities in such change.

10. **Have a fallback plan.** Sometimes events occur, almost like a stray meteor, unforeseen and random. One such may be a job loss, through no fault of your own, or a change in circumstances. It has happened to many people. It pays to have a Plan B, sufficiently thought through and ready. Otherwise, should such an event occur, it can cause you to make decisions when you are least able to do so – when you are perhaps experiencing the shock, stress and anger of what has happened. It is for this reason that people sometimes make inappropriate decisions about what to do next. Having a 'draft' Plan B in advance helps enormously in managing such a situation with clarity, direction – and even panache!

Writing your own business plan

It is time now for you to use the following template, with The Mindset of The Pioneer, and write down your own plan for success. It is important for you to commit to writing it down here or in your notebook, rather than just thinking about it in your head, so that you don't get stuck in the Swamp (you'll get round to doing it one day!). It then becomes a concrete reality and gives you your greatest chance for success.

Enjoy writing your plan... Me PLC!

BUSINESS PLAN	CAREER PLAN	MY PLAN... ME PLC
Business objectives (3-5 year period)	**Career objectives** Objectives in terms of type of work, level, industry, location and experience sought	
Business history Are the objectives realistic in terms of the business' history?	**Career progression** Patterns and achievements observable to date in your track record. Are the objectives realistic in terms of your career history?	
Background of the management team	**You** Your personal experience, responsibilities, and needs/plans for further development	
Market for the business	**Market for employment** Personal skills, qualifications, record of experience; compared with that required or expected in the market you are in	
Products	**Personal qualities & skills** What are the key aspects of your personality and skills, which could be valuable for an employer?	
Pricing policy	**Salary** What are your short- and long-term requirements? Are you prepared to accept lower earnings to acquire broad-based experience?	
Suppliers	**Employers & network** How do your current and potential employers stack up in terms of what they can offer you? How can your network help you?	
Capital assets	**Personal resources** What is your financial status? What are your commitments? Could you fund yourself through a full-time course of study? Do you have the discipline required to do evening study?	
Contingency plan (Plan B)	**Contingency plan** What will you do if you fail to achieve your objectives, or lose your present job?	

FURTHER SPACE IF NEEDED FOR NOTES

The Review: Putting it all together

'Start by doing what's necessary, then do what's possible, suddenly you are doing the impossible.'
 — St Francis of Assisi

There are people who succeed in life and work who know what fulfilment and success mean for them and how to achieve it. There are others who don't, where life and luck are always thought to be conspiring against them, where the 'system' is wrong and 'they', that is other people, hold the keys to their fate.

The difference between these two situations is, first and foremost, a mindset which is to do with being self-directing, or not, and taking Responsible Initiative for their own learning and success. The Pioneer manages their situation rather than being managed by it. They are not victims but glorious survivors.

Most people of course are neither of these extremes. Most operate in the direction of being self-directing. But we are perhaps not as 'fit' at this as we might be. For all life's pressing reasons, we often don't invest the relatively small amount of time and effort that makes the difference, not just for the work situation, but in terms of life overall. The payoff for this personal investment can be enormous, in well-being, competence and confidence, and in achieving whatever we want to achieve. This latter is of course the starting point, for everyone's definition of personal success is unique and legitimate.

This book gives you the opportunity to review and enhance both your thinking and your Skills. Both are necessary; your fate is determined by the view you take of life and work, but without certain Skills applicable to both life in general, as well as work, little will happen. These Skills are generic, and applicable to many situations, no matter what line of work or life you happen to be in. Most people have a good level of such Skills already, the idea is to build on these.

The seven Skills described in this book are the ones which make the biggest difference, and they flow through the Three Critical Steps to give you the best chance for success:

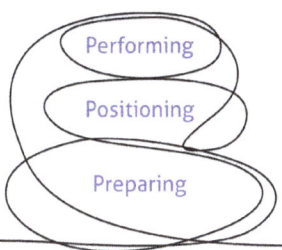

Step One: Preparing

Skill 1: Develops Personal Excellence. Shaping your own environment, shaking off any Work-Victim thoughts and being a Pioneer. You develop your own Personal Power and sense of assertion and balance; developing your Emotional Intelligence (EQ) to handle yourself and others well, and tapping into your strengths and areas of development.

Step Two: Positioning

Skill 2: Seeks Clarity – why, what and how? Appreciating good Questioning starts with Effective Listening. Doing this excellently will enable you to get the information you want and need in a manner which is both thorough and highly acceptable. Using a range of questioning techniques such as Probing, Refocusing and Critical Incident Interviewing will help you greatly.

Skill 3: Negotiates for Success. Using Positive Negotiation to enable you to get what you want, while taking other people's needs and Negotiating Styles into account, and managing conflict well using a range of powerful techniques, leading to sound conflict resolution.

Skill 4: Builds Strategic Business Acumen. This is nous: being able to see how what you are doing fits in with the bigger picture, problems are anticipated, and opportunities spotted. You pay attention to the tactical and operational aspects of your work skillfully and well. It includes being able to manage your manager.

Step Three: Performing

Skill 5: Controls Own Workload. Instead of it controlling you! This not only reduces unnecessary stress and hassle, it positions you to achieve your commitments with more grace, flow and success. You understand the behavioural traits and common timewasters that can catch you out when your resilience is low and take positive action to prevent this.

Skill 6: Manages Own Learning. Taking personal responsibility for managing your own learning and development so that your skills and abilities not only stay current and valuable but that you can stay flexible to meet new situations and opportunities. You respond well to mistakes, treating them as learning opportunities and skilfully seek and receive feedback to help you grow.

Skill 7: Takes Charge of Own Career. No one cares about this as much as you do. You are, in effect, managing your own business, which is you, even though your own business may be part of a larger one at the present time. Like any business, the starting point requires you to have a business plan and to know the strengths, weaknesses, opportunities and threats of your own business, and your own motivations.

The Pioneer Wheel

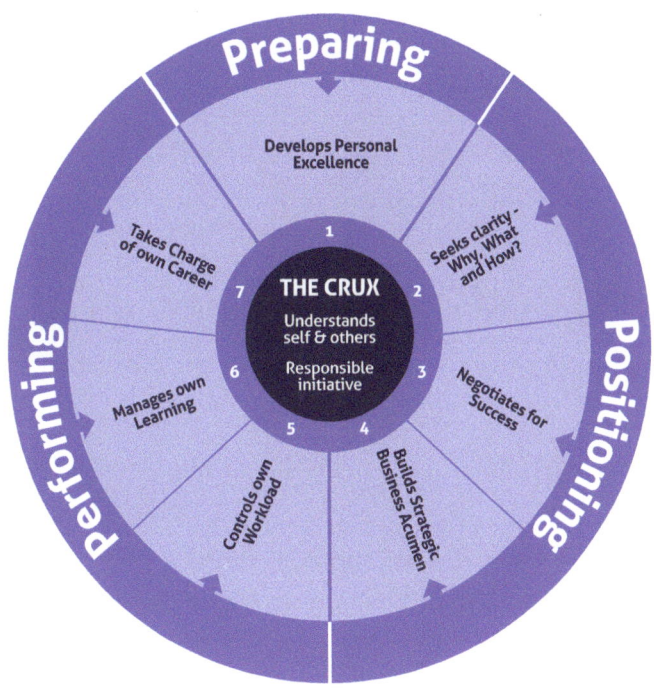

To achieve your goals in a self-directing Pioneering manner requires you to know what you want and what the definition of success is for you. You do this by having *The Pioneer* book by your side and using it to help you hone your skills and, most importantly, to write your Me PLC Plan.

All these Skills are of course Interdependent and mutually reinforce each other. They are The Pioneer Skills for life.

> 'I believe that if you'll just stand and go, life will open up for you. Something just motivates you to keep moving.'
> — Tina Turner

Chapter summary

Skill 7: Takes Charge of Own Career

The Pioneer:

- Appreciates that it is up to them to manage their own business – no one else is going to do it

- Has goals, dreams and aspirations – they have thought about their current situation and how they see things happening differently

- Understands that, if their goals are too future-oriented and general, there is a danger of being stuck in the Swamp, so they take immediate action to make their goals specific and now

- Are keenly aware of their own motivations, and how these help or hinder their current situation and future aspirations, they take action where there is any mismatch
- Commits to writing and constantly works on their own Me PLC Plan and has a fallback plan. They keep their interviewee skills current and manage change and relationships well.

The Review: Putting it all together

The Pioneer:

- Understands the self-directing Pioneering approach to work and life
- Appreciates how the Three Critical Steps and 7 Key Skills reinforce each other and lead them to being Interdependent and successful in their life and career.

'Make your life a masterpiece, imagine no limitations on what you can be, have or do.'
— Brian Tracy

Bibliography

Berne, E, *Games People Play: The psychology of human relationships* (Penguin, 2010)

Cain, S, *Quiet: The power of introverts in a world that can't stop talking* (Penguin, 2013)

Carnegie, D, *How to Win Friends and Influence People* (Pocket Books, 1998)

Cuddy, A, *Presence: Bringing your boldest self to your biggest challenges* (Little, Brown Spark, 2015)

Dweck, C, *Mindset: Changing the way you think to fulfil your potential* (Robinson, 2017)

Goleman, D, *Emotional Intelligence: Why it can matter more than IQ* (Bantam Books, 2006)

Goleman, D, *Working With Emotional Intelligence* (Bloomsbury, 1999)

Harrold, F, *Indestructible Self-Belief: 7 simple steps to getting it and keeping it* (Piatkus, 2011)

Heijligers, H, *The Anti-Procrastination Mindset: The simple art of finishing what you start* (Smart Leadership Hut, 2018)

Jacobi, Y, *The Psychology of CG Jung* (Yale University Press, 1973)

Jung, CG, *Psychological Types* (Routledge, 1971)

Kilman, RH and Thomas, KW, 'Interpersonal Conflict-Handling Behaviours as Reflections of Jungian Personality Dimensions', *Psychological Reports*, 37/3 (1975), 971–980

Robbins, A, *Awaken the Giant Within* (Simon & Schuster, 2001)

Robbins, A, *Unlimited Power: The new science of personal achievement* (Simon & Schuster, 2001)

Sharma, R, *The Leader Who Had No Title: A modern fable on real success in business and in life* (Simon & Schuster, 2010)

Sharma, R, *The Monk Who Sold His Ferrari: A fable about fulfilling your dreams and reaching your destiny* (HarperCollins, 1999)

Syed, M, *Black Box Thinking: The surprising truth about success* (John Murray, 2015)

Tracy, B, *Eat That Frog! Get more of the important things done today* (Yellow Kite, 2013)

Tracy, B, *Master Your Time, Master Your Life: The breakthrough system to get more results, faster, in every area of your life* (Tarcherperigree, 2016)

Tracy, B, *No Excuses! The power of self-discipline* (Vanguard Press, 2011)

Zander, R and Zander, B, *The Art of Possibility: Transforming professional and personal life* (Harvard Business Review Press, 2000)

Other Books In The Series

The Seeker: A clear path to developing you and your people

Ali Stewart

Are you a business owner, leader or entrepreneur... who finds managing people your biggest headache? Or maybe managing you is your biggest challenge?

If you currently lead a team, often knowing how to motivate and engage them is really hard. Some people just don't behave as you expect, some don't work well with others, some don't like their hours or pay, some consistently miss deadlines, and some cause more problems than they solve. You wonder why you bother employing people at all.

Or maybe you're the problem. You need to get out of your own way to achieve the success you deserve, and it's hard to maintain your resilience and sense of self when there's always so much to do.

This book is your perfect guide to managing you and your people. It will:

- Put you on a path to achieving more success and balance for you
- Provide you with a superb, proven system for leading people to success
- Free you up to be more strategic and do what you're good at
- Stop you becoming distracted and ground down by 'people' issues
- Enable you to keep people happy, productive and engaged

The Seeker is a light overview, combining Insights Discovery®, *The Pioneer* and *The Liberator*, into a clear 6-Point Plan for leaders and aspiring leaders. It includes case studies and stories, and is available on Amazon in hardback, paperback on Kindle and in Audio.

> 'Anyone looking to combine a leadership framework with greater self-awareness should read this book.'
> — Alex Keay, Insights UK General Manager

OTHER BOOKS IN THE SERIES

The Liberator

The Liberator: A transformational approach to leading high-performance

Ali Stewart & Dr Derek Biddle

This third book in the series forms the bedrock of our dynamic training programme. It takes leaders on a path from transactional to transformational leadership, leaving nothing to chance.

There's one thing that's certain, regardless of your business type and size: if you want to grow your business, it means leading and managing your people. The more effectively you lead, the better your team will perform and the more profitable your business will be.

Imagine you are a leader. You take your team to the top of a skyscraper and out onto the roof. The roof is flat, there are no barriers around the edge of the roof, it is dark… and the team members have roller skates on. You ask them to skate around, but they huddle together in the middle, not daring to go far. It is scary for them.

But now, if you floodlight the roof with your vision, which is so bright the team can't fail to see where they are going, and put strong railings around the edge (the clear boundaries you impose), then the team will skate to the edges, using all the space available. They know they are safe. They can try out new moves, knowing you'll catch them if they fall. They will put on a magnificent display, exceeding all your expectations.

To achieve this clarity of purpose, to shine the light authentically and to set the boundaries, a leader needs a specific Mindset and set of Skills. Anyone can learn them. You don't need exceptional characteristics, a high IQ or a degree in human resources.

This book leads you through the process, helping you become a truly liberated leader of people.

> 'For me, the Liberating Leadership programme brought together years of teaching and learning around leadership development in one place – a real gem!'
> — Paul Thompson, Owner, Westminster Associates Ltd

These books are available on Amazon, Kindle and Audio.

OTHER BOOKS IN THE SERIES

Ask us for information on the supporting coaching programme, The Liberator Programme – a nine-month programme that takes you on a journey from self-discovery to self-mastery, to being able to lead and develop people to consistently outstanding levels of performance. You will lead with more strength, dignity and compassion.

www.alistewartandco.com/programmes

> 'Leadership is lifting a person's vision to higher sights; the raising of a person's performance to a higher standard; the building of a personality beyond its normal limitations.'
> — Peter F Drucker

Next Steps: The Pioneer Programme

The Pioneer Programme is an 18-week programme helping you to explore how to take your untapped talent and use it to propel your career to the next level.

We help you to build the Mindset and Skills described in *The Pioneer* to manage your career effectively, conquer your workload, negotiate for success, and build powerful relationships that will accelerate your growth.

To lead others, you need to first lead your own professional development. We help you become an unstoppable Pioneer for yourself and pave the way to the next step – which is to liberate others.

All the information you need can be found here:

www.alistewartandco.com/programmes

Contact us for a chat:

http://alistewartandco.com/contact

Or email us here: letstalk@alistewartandco.com

Acknowledgements

To all professionals willing to work on their Mindset and Skills to become Pioneering in every way.

We honour the fact you are reading this book and are taking the initiative to develop your Pioneering spirit.

It is not easy and requires you to try and try again, using the tools and processes contained in this book to help you on your way.

Thank you to our friends and colleagues over time who have helped with the development of our thinking. There are so many we don't want to offend by missing any names. You know who you are, and we hope you will love this latest version of the book.

The Authors

Ali Stewart

Ali is a masterful leadership coach. Also a mentor, best-selling author, Master NLP Practitioner, Fellow of the Association for Coaching, and an unmistakable force in her field.

Having already built a thriving management consultancy, Ali founded Ali Stewart & Co. in July 2004. She's been a guiding light for hundreds of leaders from a whole range of industries, helping them make their mark and become exceptional in their field.

In 2008, she founded the accrediting body for The Liberator and The Pioneer programmes, and it's been growing ever since. With over 300 practitioners accredited worldwide, Ali, together with her team, hopes to welcome even more into the fold. Especially trainers, coaches, leaders and HR professionals who would like to use these models to turbocharge both their growth and that of their clients or teams.

What drives Ali? A heartfelt desire to see every leader on the planet make developing people their number one priority... and for individuals to get out of their own way and allow their natural brilliance to shine.

She lives in the South of England with her husband. They have three children, and currently three grandchildren and two cats. She has a passion for music, baking and family.

Derek Biddle PhD

Initially training as a Chartered Engineer and while working at a paper mill in New Zealand, Derek became increasingly interested in the human aspect of the process. And so his study of people began.

On his return to the UK, he then trained as a Chartered Occupational Psychologist and HR Professional, assuming many senior leadership positions in major organisations, including Roffey Park Management College.

With Ali, Derek founded Stratagem Human Resources in 1992, working with many significant organisations, including the Foreign & Commonwealth Office, Friends

Provident (now Friends Life), Sunseeker, South West Water, Severn Trent Water and General Motors. It was in these organisations, and many more like them who had graduate programmes in place, where The Pioneer approach was researched, captured and refined, with great success.

Derek's early training as an engineer gives this self-directing approach a distinct and logical structure, turning what many view as 'soft skills' into a clear strategy. He was delighted when discovering the success of highfliers had nothing to do with having a high IQ, and had more to do with having a high EQ (Emotional Quotient or Intelligence) – which means anyone can learn the skills and be high flying if they choose to be.

Derek helped Ali establish the accreditation programme for coaches, trainers and consultants, before fully retiring in about 2007. As a seasoned sailor, Derek enjoys being out on his boat, and he has taught himself to play the banjo.